CONNECTED RIGHTS: REIMAGINING HUMAN FREEDOM IN THE DIGITAL AGE

PREFACE

In an age where one's presence online can be as telling as one's physical footprint, the conversation surrounding human rights has evolved into uncharted territory. As I reflect on the issues in "Connected Rights: Reimagining Human Freedom in the Digital Age," I am compelled by the sheer magnitude and urgency of advocating for internet access as a fundamental human right. This book emerges from years of research and introspection, guided by a personal commitment to exploring how digital connectivity transforms our daily lives, our societies, and our understanding of freedom itself.

My journey into this digital discourse began in the quiet hours spent as an academic, engrossed in the history and philosophy of human rights. As the digital world burgeoned, I found myself at a crossroads, witnessing technology's double-edged impact: its unparalleled potential to democratize information and opportunity, and its propensity to exacerbate existing inequalities. These insights demanded an exploration of rights through a digital lens, prompting an urgent narrative about reconciling traditional freedom with the complexities of the digital age.

The inspiration behind this book was further fueled by encounters and stories from individuals across the globe, who navigate these digital terrains daily. From students in rural areas leveraging limited connectivity to access education, to technologists advocating for privacy in an era of surveillance, their voices illuminate the power and pitfalls of our digital evolution. This book, therefore, seeks to bridge these experiences with scholarly analysis, serving as both a reflection and roadmap, one that underscores the need for equitable internet access as a moral imperative.

I am deeply honored to offer this analysis, woven with a profound intention to engage, enlighten, and empower. My professional quest is not merely to inform but to transform, to reshape perspectives and incite dialogue that can fuel policy change, enabling a future where digital inclusion is universally recognized and accessible. Through the chapters in this book, I hope to bring readers to a fulcrum of understanding, where philosophy, law, ethics, and technology converge to mold our comprehensions of rights in this rapidly transforming world.

"Connected Rights" draws on rich interactions with colleagues, experts, and communities that lent their voices and knowledge to this critical dialogue. This collaboration and shared vision lie at the heart of this work, aiming to create a collective compass guiding us toward a digitally inclusive society.

I sincerely hope that through this book, readers will imbibe a renewed appreciation of digital rights and discover the impetus to pursue, question, and advocate for a world where freedom is inclusive of digital equity. Regardless of one's background or digital proficiency, my aspiration is that each reader will embrace the opportunity to contribute toward a global understanding and commitment to protecting these emergent rights in meaningful ways.

As you turn these pages, may you find both the inspiration and the tools to engage with the digital rights movement, compelled not by the digital transformation alone, but by the human faces and freedoms it affects.

TABLE OF CONTENTS

INTRODUCTION: RE-DEFINING FREEDOM IN THE DIGITAL ERA

In an era defined by bytes and bandwidth, the paradox of connection and isolation paints a vivid landscape where the concept of freedom dares to be reimagined. As we step into this digital epoch, the pathways of human rights traverse not merely through parchments and proclamations but through fiber-optic cables and satellites. The symphony of ones and zeros heralds a new dawn of access and agency, forging a world where the digital realm becomes the battleground for rights, equality, and opportunity.

When the world was connected to the internet for the first time, no one envisioned the profound impact it would have on our understanding of freedom and rights. What began as an innovation to enhance communication has grown into an essential infrastructure for learning, working, socializing, and mobilizing for social justice. In this landscape, where almost every aspect of our lives is touched by digital technology, the question arises: should access to the internet be considered a fundamental human right?

The answer begins with a journey back in time. The history

of human rights is one of continuous evolution. From the Magna Carta to the Universal Declaration of Human Rights, society has progressively expanded the definition of rights to match the needs of the time. Our forebears could scarcely have imagined a world where information flows across continents in milliseconds, or where the digital divide could determine one's ability to participate fully in modern life. Today, we are called upon to once again extend our understanding of rights to ensure the progress we champion includes everyone.

Internet access is far more than a mere facet of modern life; it is the backbone of contemporary existence, a medium through which the most fundamental of human rights are exercised. Freedom of expression, access to education, even the ability to freely assemble and share grievances , all rest upon the robust and unfettered access to digital networks. Recognizing internet access as a basic human right, therefore, is not simply a notion of convenience but a necessity for ensuring economic and social justice. The implications of this recognition are profound, impacting legal frameworks, ethical standards, and governmental responsibilities on a global scale.

Throughout this book, we are tasked with examining the myriad ways in which digital connectivity alters the landscape of rights and freedoms. We delve into the historical progression of human rights, exploring the philosophical foundations that guide our understanding of what it means for a right to be 'digital.' The narrative investigates the transformative power of technology not just as a tool but as a catalyst for empowerment and agency, while; at the same time noting the potential pitfalls of such reliance. We explore how existing legal frameworks navigate the challenges posed by digital expansions and how ethical considerations must permeate the dialogue surrounding privacy, surveillance, and data ownership.

Consider the village of Fictoria, a community nestled between the mountains, overlooked by traditional infrastructure development. Here, digital access changes lives. Sarah, a young mother of three, runs her online business while her children attend virtual school; opportunities that enhance their lives immeasurably. Meanwhile, in the bustling metropolis of Metropolis City, the lack of digital access for underserved populations perpetuates cycles of poverty and social immobility. These stories, synthesized from real experiences but anonymized for discretion, illustrate the power of connectivity to break barriers and foster social and economic equity.

Yet, the disparity in digital access underscores the importance of addressing digital equity. Bridging the digital divide is not a mere act of benevolence but a critical investment in our shared future. By understanding and addressing these global disparities, we enable the transformative potential of the internet to be felt by all , uniting communities, facilitating socioeconomic development, and enacting positive societal change.

Through the inspiring tales of individuals and communities that have leveraged digital access to enhance their lives, we witness the internet's words not only through data but through stories of resilience and innovation. From grassroots organizations fostering digital literacy in remote areas to policymakers crafting initiatives that promote equitable access, these case studies illustrate the power of connectivity to drive change.

Moreover, the role of governments and corporations cannot be understated. They are the architects of the digital infrastructure, the stewards of policy and the gatekeepers of access. Their responsibilities, challenges, and potential solutions form a crucial part of the dialogue, as we explore policy interventions and partnerships that can bring the goal of universal internet access to fruition. The economic implications of connectivity are vast, influencing markets, employment opportunities, and even geopolitical dynamics.

As we weave through the insights of scholars, technologists, and activists, we contemplate the future. Digital rights are evolving, and with them, the conception of citizenship transcends geographic boundaries, offering a new vision of inclusivity and mobilization. This forward-looking perspective on digital rights invites us to imagine, to innovate, and to advocate for a future where connectivity is not a privilege of a few, but a right of all.

Ultimately, "Connected Rights: Reimagining Human Freedom in the Digital Age" is more than an exploration of digital rights; it is a call to action. Dr. Eleanor Rees invites readers to engage with the possibility of a world where digital access transforms lives and rights are as interconnected as the world they inhabit. It is a clarion call for inclusion, challenging each reader to reflect on their role in shaping a digital future where connectivity is a universal reality, and human freedom is indivisibly linked with digital rights. The journey of understanding and transformation begins here, guiding readers to engage with the digital age's challenges and opportunities with clarity, purpose, and hope.

CHAPTER 1: THE EVOLUTION OF HUMAN RIGHTS

In a world constantly redefined by the ebb and flow of global change, one concept has persistently stood as a beacon for justice: human rights. As we embark on this exploration of the ever-evolving narrative of human rights, we are reminded of the axioms that transcend time, the intrinsic values, freedoms, and dignities that bind us all in a shared vision of humanity. This chapter sets the groundwork for understanding how human rights have transformed from early theoretical musings into the unparalleled frameworks that shape modern governance, influence cultural dynamics, and challenge the boundaries of what it means to be human in a digital age.

The story begins at the genesis of human rights concepts, where the philosophical seeds of individual liberty and dignity took root in iconic documents such as the Magna Carta and the Declaration of the Rights of Man. Subchapter 1 delves into this fertile historical soil to uncover the intellectual and political forces that heralded an era of transformative thought. By examining these foundational texts, Dr. Eleanor Rees illustrates the crystallization of protection for inherent human dignity, setting the stage for the monumental shifts to come.

With the dawn of the twentieth century came the acceleration of these ideas onto a new stage, the international arena. In Subchapter 2, we trace the burgeoning growth of global human rights frameworks. It was during this period that visionary agreements like the Universal Declaration of Human Rights took center stage, aspiring to bridge the vast array of cultural and political landscapes with a universal set of principles. Dr. Rees deftly navigates the challenges and milestones of these endeavors, offering insights into the tensions and triumphs that have shaped the modern human rights discourse.

To move forward, we must acknowledge the undeniable impact of social movements in demanding and achieving expanded rights. In Subchapter 3, the influence of collective action comes to the fore. From civil rights to gender equality, social justice movements have been instrumental in expanding the scope of what society deems as fundamental rights. Through compelling case studies, this section reveals how these movements, powered by resolute individuals, have dynamically redefined the landscape of human rights, advocating for more inclusion and equity.

A modern discourse on human rights would be incomplete without addressing the profound implications of technology. Subchapter 4 examines how digital advancements pose both opportunities and perils for individual freedoms. As Dr. Rees explores, technology's double-edged sword raises pivotal questions for traditional notions of rights, questions that are both timely and necessary as we grapple with issues of digital privacy, surveillance, and the empowerment technology can afford.

Finally, with an eye toward the horizon, Subchapter 5 lays the groundwork for recognizing digital connectivity as an emergent human right. This discussion signals a seamless transition into the core themes of the book, offering a critical examination of the nascent digital rights movement. Dr. Rees invites readers to consider how connectivity sits within this continuum, challenging us to envision a future where online access is as fundamental as the rights conceived centuries ago.

As we traverse this chapter, remember: the evolution of human rights is not just a chronicle of past achievements, but an ongoing journey toward justice and equity in an increasingly interconnected world.

Subchapter 1: The Birth of Human Rights Concepts

Human rights, as they are understood today, are the culmination of centuries of philosophical debates and political developments. The roots of these ideals stretch deep into history, originating from a collective human yearning for justice and dignity. In this subchapter, we explore the historical emergence of human rights as a concept, tracing their philosophical and political journey through seminal documents and the thinkers who crafted them.

The story of human rights begins not with a single doctrine or document, but rather as a tapestry woven through time, influenced by diverse cultures and perspectives. The Magna Carta, signed in 1215, stands as one of the earliest frameworks advancing the notion of individual liberties against autocratic power. Although primarily a political agreement between King John of England and his barons, the Magna Carta established critical principles that would echo through the ages: the rule of law and the idea that the sovereign is not above the law.

This revolutionary document planted the seeds of personal freedom, sowing an enduring belief that individuals have intrinsic rights that even rulers must respect. Centuries later, the English Bill of Rights of 1689 built upon these foundations, further delineating citizens' rights and the limitations of sovereign power. It highlighted concepts such as free speech within Parliament, the right to petition the monarch, and the prohibition of cruel and unusual punishment, concepts that resonate with modern human rights standards.

Across the Channel, the Declaration of the Rights of Man and of the Citizen, adopted during the French Revolution in 1789, articulated the universal and indivisible nature of rights. This ambitious document declared liberty, property, security, and resistance to oppression as fundamental human rights. Notably, it emphasized equality before the law and articulated the idea that political power should derive from the nation's general will, rather than divine right or tradition.

The philosophical underpinnings of these documents reflect broader intellectual currents that shaped their creation. The Enlightenment, a period of profound intellectual flourishing in the 17th and 18th centuries, offered fertile ground for the germination of ideas about individual rights. Key Enlightenment thinkers, such as John Locke, Jean-Jacques Rousseau, and Montesquieu, contributed significantly to the development of human rights philosophy.

John Locke's theory of natural rights, detailed in his seminal work "Two Treatises of Government," proposed that individuals inherently possess rights to life, liberty, and property. Locke argued that governments exist primarily to protect these rights, and if they fail, citizens have the right to revolt. This radical notion of a social contract between the government and its people laid the groundwork for modern democratic systems and the contemporary understanding of rights as inherent and inalienable.

Meanwhile, Rousseau's concept of the general will, introduced in "The Social Contract," asserted that true freedom requires individuals to participate actively in the collective governing process. Rousseau's ideas inspired revolutionary movements around the world, underscoring the relationship between individual rights and collective sovereignty.

Montesquieu, with his advocacy for the separation of powers, argued for a political system that prevents the concentration of power and facilitates the protection of freedoms. His insights greatly influenced the framers of the United States Constitution and subsequent democratic structures worldwide.

As we reflect on these critical milestones, it becomes evident that the ideological development of human rights was not confined to Western thought alone. Across the world, diverse traditions contributed to the evolving discourse on human dignity. In the Indian subcontinent, the Buddhist King Ashoka, who ruled in the 3rd century BCE, established edicts promoting social welfare, non-violence, and religious tolerance, which resonate with contemporary human rights principles.

Similarly, in China, Confucian and Taoist philosophies emphasized harmony, respect for others, and the moral responsibilities of rulers toward their subjects. These values, though framed differently from Western notions of rights, underscored the universal human aspiration for social justice and dignity.

Bringing these philosophical and historical narratives into contemporary focus, we find that the collective impulses that gave birth to human rights continue to inspire action and reform. Consider the current global struggle for gender equality, a reflection of centuries-old debates on personal and civic rights. In Saudi Arabia, where women have long been subject to restrictive guardianship laws, recent reforms have granted women the right to drive, travel, and participate more freely in civil society. These changes, while gradual, illustrate the enduring relevance of the human rights discourse in modern society.

Let us consider a practical scenario that encapsulates the ongoing evolution of human rights: the case of marriage equality in the United States. It serves as a contemporary illustration of how historical principles of human dignity and equality are applied to challenge and redefine societal norms. In the landmark case Obergefell v. Hodges in 2015, the U.S. Supreme Court ruled that the fundamental right to marry is guaranteed to same-sex couples. This decision, deeply rooted in the earlier philosophical and legal traditions we have explored, underscored the universal applicability of human rights to new social realities.

By examining these historical and philosophical trajectories, readers can better appreciate the profound impact that the ideals of personal liberty and justice have had on shaping the modern world. The evolution of human rights concepts is not merely an academic exercise but a living dialogue, constantly reimagining how society acknowledges and protects individual dignity. This ongoing journey, influenced by historical precedents and diverse cultural philosophies, remains a testament to humanity's relentless pursuit of freedom and justice. As we transition to the next section, where we explore the formalization of these ideals into international frameworks, the foundational insights examined here will illuminate the challenges and triumphs in codifying rights on a global scale.

Subchapter 2: The Growth of International Human Rights Frameworks

The dawn of the twentieth century marked an era of significant shifts in the recognition and protection of human rights, particularly on the international stage. As nations began to grasp the concept of a shared moral and ethical obligation toward all humans, the groundwork was laid for establishing cohesive standards that transcended borders. In this subchapter, we delve into the proliferation of global agreements and institutions dedicated to human rights protections, analyzing their attempts to offer universal standards while contending with the diverse tapestry of cultures and political ideologies.

The first vital milestone in constructing a universal human rights architecture was the adoption of the Universal Declaration of Human Rights (UDHR) in 1948. After the harrowing events of World War II, there was a palpable global urge to codify a set of rights that would serve as a safeguard against atrocities like those witnessed during the conflict. The United Nations, newly formed, became the vessel through which these ideals were realized. The UDHR's creation marked a watershed moment in history, as it articulated a comprehensive set of rights and freedoms to which all individuals are entitled. Its preamble and 30 articles provided a roadmap for what it means to afford dignity and respect universally, covering civil, political, economic, social, and cultural rights.

However, the implementation of the UDHR was not without its challenges. The initial enthusiasm for universal rights brought to light significant tensions, particularly as the Cold War era emerged. The ideological clash between the Eastern bloc, spearheaded by the Soviet Union, and the Western powers, primarily led by the United States and its allies, highlighted the difficulties of creating truly universal standards. While the Western nations championed civil and political rights, such as freedom of speech and the right to a fair trial, the Soviet bloc emphasized economic, social, and cultural rights, including the right to work and education. This division resulted in the eventual creation of two separate covenants in 1966: the International Covenant on Civil and Political Rights (ICCPR) and the International Covenant on Economic, Social and Cultural Rights (ICESCR). Together, these documents, alongside the UDHR, comprise the International Bill of Human Rights, underpinning all subsequent human rights laws and treaties.

One of the primary aims of these documents was to establish a framework through which nations could be held accountable. Yet, as Dr. Eleanor Rees meticulously explores, despite their promise, compliance remained, and still remains, a significant issue. Enforcement mechanisms were originally weak, and without a binding international court with comprehensive jurisdiction, ensuring adherence largely relied on peer pressure and diplomatic influence. This has led to a patchwork success rate in the application of international human rights standards, where some nations have embraced these concepts more fully than others.

A practical illustration of both the challenges and triumphs in implementing international human rights frameworks can be found in South Africa. In the latter half of the 20th century, the country was embroiled in the brutal apartheid regime, characterized by institutionalized racial segregation and discrimination. The anti-apartheid movement gained momentum partly due to the international community's increased emphasis on human rights. Global entities such as the United Nations levied sanctions and international pressure, condemning South Africa's policies and aligning these efforts with the principles espoused in the UDHR and ICCPR. Eventually, the compounded internal resistance and international ostracism led to the dismantling of apartheid, culminating in the democratic election of Nelson Mandela in 1994. This scenario effectively illustrates how international human rights frameworks can influence and accelerate change, yet also demonstrates the necessity of internal momentum and the limitations of external pressure alone.

Despite these achievements, the international framework often struggled with the universality of application, colliding head-on with the concept of state sovereignty and cultural relativism. Dr. Rees emphasizes that nations often pointed to their unique cultural contexts to argue against the imposition of universal human rights standards, posing the question: should universal principles always override local traditions and customs? A notable example of this ongoing debate can be seen in discussions surrounding women's rights and gender equality. While international conventions like the Convention on the Elimination of All Forms of Discrimination Against Women (CEDAW) aim to eradicate gender-based discrimination worldwide, many nations, citing cultural and religious justifications, resist adopting particular provisions.

The situation in Saudi Arabia, for instance, has historically highlighted the tension between global human rights expectations and local customs. Women in the kingdom were long denied many fundamental rights, such as the ability to drive or travel without male guardianship, despite global critique. However, the advent of Vision 2030, a strategic initiative by the Saudi government to reform and diversify its economy, partly in response to global pressures and economic imperatives, has prompted significant, albeit gradual, changes in women's rights. The changes included lifting the driving ban and easing the male guardianship law, showcasing how international frameworks can catalyze change over time, even in deeply resistant settings.

Beyond treaties and conventions, the 20th century also saw the formation of specialized institutions to monitor and address human rights violations globally. The establishment of bodies such as the Human Rights Council and the Office of the High Commissioner for Human Rights has played a critical role in documenting abuses and advocating for victims. These institutions have increased global awareness and provided platforms for addressing grievances, launching inquiries, and enabling non-governmental organizations to magnify their calls for justice. Dr. Rees contends that these institutions act as both watchdogs and ambassadors for human rights, albeit often hindered by political constraints and the immense scale of global issues requiring attention.

In recent years, these frameworks have faced new challenges, including the rise of populist governments that contest international influence and critique multilateralism. Leaders in countries such as the United States, Hungary, and Brazil have at times eschewed international norms, reasserting national sovereignty in ways that undermine collaborative efforts to uphold human rights. Such dynamics have necessitated a reevaluation of strategies among human rights advocates, compelling them to innovate and adapt their approaches in an evolving geopolitical environment.

Nevertheless, the growth of international human rights frameworks remains a testament to an enduring collective ideal: the belief in the intrinsic worth of every human being. For these ideals to translate into reality, they must not only be enshrined in international documents but also ingrained in national policies, societal norms, and everyday actions. A practical application of these frameworks can be seen in how international human rights agreements are incorporated into national constitutions and legal systems. Countries such as Canada and Sweden have successfully integrated international human rights standards into their domestic legislation, serving as models for legal transposition and domestic accountability.

As we move forward into the subsequent subchapter, the impact of social movements on human rights expansion becomes a focal point. While legal structures and institutional frameworks provide the foundation, it is often grassroots action and social advocacy that propel human rights issues into the public consciousness, challenging existing paradigms and fostering change from the ground up. Through the lens of these movements, Dr. Rees will further explore how collective action continues to reshape our understanding and implementation of human rights across the globe.

Subchapter 3: The Impact of Social Movements on Human Rights Expansion

The landscape of human rights is not static; it is an ever-evolving tapestry woven through advocacy and the deep, resonant cries for justice that have echoed across centuries. Among the most significant drivers of change and expansion in the realm of human rights are the social movements that have emerged worldwide. These movements have not merely reacted against injustices but have proactively reimagined the parameters of what constitutes a 'right.' By translating often abstract ideals into actionable reforms, social movements have redefined the boundaries of human rights, making them increasingly inclusive and reflective of diverse human experiences.

One of the most compelling aspects of social movements is their ability to elevate marginalized voices and challenge entrenched power structures. The Civil Rights Movement in the United States is an illustrative example of how collective action can forge significant breakthroughs in the realm of human rights. This movement, led by figures like Martin Luther King Jr. and Rosa Parks, among others, leveraged nonviolent protests, legal challenges, and the power of storytelling to dismantle institutionalized racial segregation and discrimination. The movement's impact is palpable, having paved the way for landmark legislation such as the Civil Rights Act of 1964 and the Voting Rights Act of 1965. These historic legal shifts underscored the notion that equality and justice are non-negotiable rights for all, regardless of race or background.

In tandem, the struggle for gender equality has similarly inched forward, driven by the relentless efforts of feminist movements across the globe. From the suffragettes of the early 20th century to contemporary advocates for gender parity, the fight for women's rights has catalyzed profound societal changes. One notable milestone is the inclusion of gender equality as a fundamental human right in international frameworks, such as the Convention on the Elimination of All Forms of Discrimination Against Women (CEDAW) adopted by the United Nations in 1979. This international treaty has been instrumental in advocating for the rights of women and ensuring legislative reforms in numerous countries to promote equality in areas such as education, employment, and reproductive health.

Furthermore, social movements have not been confined to nation-states; many have transcended borders to espouse universal causes, illustrating the interconnectedness of human rights issues. The LGBTQ+ rights movement, for instance, began in small, localized efforts advocating for recognition and equality. Over the decades, it has burgeoned into a global crusade, advancing issues such as marriage equality and anti-discrimination protections. The legalization of same-sex marriage in various parts of the world, beginning with the Netherlands in 2001, is a testament to the power of sustained activism rooted in resilience and an unwavering conviction in the right to love freely.

The environmental movement is another poignant example of how grassroots mobilization has instigated a shift in the perception of rights. Spearheaded by individuals like Rachel Carson, whose seminal work "Silent Spring" ignited a new consciousness about the interdependencies of ecosystems and human health, this movement has slowly but effectively embedded environmental protection within the purview of human rights. This expansion recognizes the right to a clean and sustainable environment as intrinsic to the well-being of individuals and communities, a perspective increasingly reflected in international declarations and local legislation.

Each social movement offers its unique narratives and lessons that reverberate beyond their immediate contexts. The strength of these movements lies not only in their ability to challenge and alter legal statutes or political regimes but also in their capacity to effectuate a profound cultural transformation. They inspire and galvanize future generations, advocating that the measure of society's progress is inextricably linked to its capacity to accommodate and uplift all of its constituents, irrespective of their identity or status.

A particularly pertinent case study highlighting the power of social movements in advancing human rights can be seen in the recent advocacy efforts surrounding disability rights. Historically, individuals with disabilities have faced systemic exclusion and invisibility, confined by societal barriers that curtail their autonomy and participation. However, the disability rights movement has sought to rectify these disparities through initiatives like the Americans with Disabilities Act (ADA) in the United States, ensuring access and equality in various sectors, from employment to transportation.

More globally, the Convention on the Rights of Persons with Disabilities (CRPD), adopted by the United Nations in 2006, marked a significant shift in global policies, urging nation-states to recognize and uphold the rights of persons with disabilities comprehensively. By reframing disability within the context of human rights rather than solely a medical or charitable domain, this movement underscores the dignity and agency of individuals, advocating for an inclusive societal structure that honors diversity.

The ongoing dialogue around rights and responsibilities reflects a dynamic interplay between historical legacies and contemporary realities, adapting to the needs and aspirations of diverse constituencies. As society continues to grapple with new challenges, the lessons gleaned from past movements offer both a foundation and an impetus for ongoing advocacy.

As this discourse transitions to subsequent discussions on technological advances and their implications, they serve as a reminder of the power of collective action and the importance of maintaining a vigilant, informed, and adaptable approach to human rights advocacy. This approach must align itself with emerging facets of modern life, including digital rights and the critical role technology plays in shaping future paradigms of equity and freedom.

Practical Example:

Consider the case of the Arab Spring, which began in 2010 as a series of anti-government protests across the Arab world. Catalyzed by societal disenfranchisement and economic injustice, these movements rapidly garnered international attention, shedding light on the intersection of human rights and political freedoms. Social media platforms like Twitter and Facebook emerged as powerful tools for organization and communication, transcending traditional barriers and underscoring technology's role in modern activism.

However, while the movements achieved varying degrees of success in toppling authoritarian regimes, they also highlighted the complex interplay between digital technology, censorship, and state power. This duality reflects modern social movements' capacities to redefine human rights frameworks, through both grass-root actions and the technologies they harness. As we step into subsequent discussions on digital rights within the broader human rights continuum, the lessons of the Arab Spring offer critical insights into how these movements can amplify voices, connect individuals, and instigate lasting change.

Subchapter 4: Technological Intrusions and Their Implications on Rights

In the vibrant, rapidly changing tapestry of our global society, technology interweaves with every thread, commanding profound transformations across social, economic, and political realms. History reveals that each technological revolution, from the printing press to the internet, significantly impacts human rights. As we progress through the 21st century, digital technology assumes a pivotal role, reshaping the landscape of rights and raising critical questions about their definition, protection, and evolution.

The Dual Edge of Digital Technology

Digital technology embodies a quintessential paradox: it wields the power to liberate yet simultaneously constrain. On the one hand, digital tools have democratized access to information, empowered marginalized communities, and facilitated global connectivity. On the other, they introduce complexities around privacy, surveillance, and exploitation. Dr. Eleanor Rees eloquently encapsulates this duality, asserting that while technology can amplify voices that were previously unheard, it also poses the risk of infringing on personal freedoms.

Consider the example of the Arab Spring, where social media platforms like Facebook and Twitter became catalysts for political change. Activists utilized these platforms to mobilize support, spread awareness, and document injustices, effectively challenging authoritarian regimes. This digital empowerment exemplified the unprecedented reach and influence of technology on society and human rights. However, the same platforms can be co-opted by state actors or malicious entities to surveil, censor, and manipulate citizens, underscoring the delicate balance between empowerment and control.

Surveillance and Privacy: A Delicate Balance

With the proliferation of digital ecosystems, surveillance has become increasingly sophisticated and pervasive. Governments now possess the capability to engage in mass data collection, often justifying it under the pretext of national security. This surveillance extends to tracking online activities, monitoring communications, and even predicting behaviors based on algorithms. While the intent may be to safeguard citizens, it raises poignant questions about privacy, consent, and the potential for abuse of power.

Edward Snowden's revelations about the National Security Agency's extensive surveillance operations in the United States highlighted the tension between security and privacy. These disclosures sparked international debate, emphasizing the need to reconcile state security interests with individual rights. The global reaction underscored that as technology continues to evolve, so must our frameworks for protecting rights in digital spaces, ensuring they are not sacrificed at the altar of progress.

The Challenge of Algorithmic Discrimination

Amidst these developments, the rise of artificial intelligence and machine learning further complicate the human rights debate. Algorithms, though inherently neutral, can perpetuate biases present in their training data. This perpetuation can lead to discriminatory outcomes that significantly impact the lives of individuals and communities, particularly those already marginalized.

A pertinent example is the use of algorithmic decision-making in the criminal justice system, where tools are designed to assess the risk of reoffending. Critiques argue that these algorithms often reflect existing societal prejudices, disproportionately affecting people of color who may receive harsher sentencing based on biased data inputs. Such scenarios demand a reevaluation of accountability and fairness within technological systems, urging society to scrutinize and refine these tools to uphold human rights without prejudice.

Digital Exploitation: A Growing Concern

The digital age also ushers in new forms of exploitation, notably concerning labor rights in the gig economy and the proliferation of digital trafficking. Laborers in the gig economy confront challenges related to fair compensation, job security, and working conditions due to the decentralized nature of digital platforms. These platforms often evade traditional labor regulations, compromising workers' rights and benefits.

Moreover, the anonymity of digital spaces facilitates illicit activities, from human trafficking to child exploitation. The dark web provides a haven for such acts, obstructing justice and accountability. Combating these issues requires robust international cooperation and the development of digital literacy, empowering users to identify and report exploitative behaviors effectively.

Cybersecurity: Protecting a Rights-Based Internet

With the stakes higher than ever, ensuring cybersecurity is paramount to sustaining a rights-based internet. Cyberattacks, whether on individual or state levels, can disrupt crucial services, invade personal privacy, and threaten national security. Strengthening cybersecurity measures thus becomes essential to safeguarding human rights in the digital realm.

In December 2020, a significant breach exposed vulnerabilities in cybersecurity infrastructure, affecting multiple governments and organizations. The incident underscored the need for comprehensive strategies to defend against cyber threats. An international approach, characterized by collaboration and shared expertise, is vital to fortifying digital defenses and maintaining the sanctity of rights online.

Practical Application: The Promise of Blockchain Technology

In response to these challenges, innovations like blockchain technology offer promising avenues for enhancing rights protection. Blockchain, a decentralized ledger system, champions transparency and accountability, addressing issues from integrity in financial transactions to secure information sharing.

Consider its application in securing land rights in Honduras, where blockchain has been piloted to prevent false land claims and corruption. By ensuring records remain tamper-proof and reliably accessible, blockchain technology strengthens property rights, a fundamental human right, especially in regions vulnerable to exploitative practices.

As humanity stands on the precipice of an unprecedented digital era, careful navigation through these technological evolutions is imperative. In reaffirming human rights as an inextricable part of the digital dialogue, we must also recognize the need for responsible stewardship of technology to protect and uplift global citizens. On this journey, the ensuing discussion in Subchapter 5 will pave the way for exploring digital rights recognition, advocating for an interconnected world where connectivity is equitable and universally accessible.

Subchapter 5: Laying the Groundwork for Digital Rights Recognition

As we stand on the brink of an era increasingly defined by digital connectivity, the urgent call to recognize internet access as a fundamental human right is gaining undeniable momentum. This subchapter navigates the initial strides taken in embedding digital connectivity alongside traditional human rights, enabling readers to observe the iterative process of rights evolution in a modern context. Through the explorations of early advocacy, policy frameworks, and initiative-based solutions, we will traverse the path leading to the potential enshrinement of digital rights as critical tenets of human dignity and societal progress.

The Dawn of Digital Rights Advocacy

The journey toward recognizing digital inclusion as a human right has historical parallels with earlier rights expansions, often born out of necessity and driven by pioneering foresight. In the early 2000s, as digital innovations began to reshape communication, economy, and governance structures, forward-thinking advocates recognized the nascent potential and pitfalls of unequal digital access. Pioneering voices such as Vinton Cerf, one of the internet's founding fathers, argued passionately that internet access should be considered a civil right, an essential utility akin to public education or healthcare.

Responding to the early advocates' clarion calls, several international and national initiatives began to sprout. The drive was to ensure that the internet, initially viewed as a privilege of more affluent societies, became a democratized tool for empowerment. Insights from global bodies like the World Summit on the Information Society (WSIS) highlighted a growing consensus: bridging the digital divide was vital not only for technical advancement but also for the holistic development of societies.

Supporting this assertion, the then United Nations Secretary-General, Kofi Annan, emphasized the transformative power of information technologies in achieving development goals and fostering social inclusion. Annan's vision set a tone of urgency and optimism, leading to foundational discussions in forums dedicated to global cooperation on digital access and rights, such as the Internet Governance Forum.

Pilot Initiatives and Policy Frameworks

With advocacy strong at its core, experimental pilot initiatives around the globe sought to bridge the existing digital chasms. Some regional governments were quick to respond; nations such as Finland took unprecedented steps by legislating internet access as a legal right. By 2010, Finland became the first country to make broadband access a right for every citizen, representing a groundbreaking acknowledgment of digital inclusion as a societal cornerstone.

Finland's initiative served as a beacon for other countries, igniting policy debates and legislative actions in various regions. For instance, in Estonia, access to the internet was declared a human right, recognizing early that connectivity was essential for citizen engagement in digital government services and awareness. These groundbreaking policy moves provided invaluable insights into the operationalization of digital rights, emphasizing adaptability to cultural and infrastructural contexts.

Globally, multi-stakeholder initiatives such as the Alliance for Affordable Internet (A4AI) were established, aiming to lower the financial barriers to internet access while fostering sustainable models of connectivity. Through cross-sector collaborations, these initiatives worked to establish actionable frameworks to ensure that not only were networks expanded, but that users could effectively harness the opportunities presented by digital access.

The Role of Emerging Economies and NGOs

As high-income countries experimented with policy and legislative approaches to digital access, emerging economies and non-governmental organizations (NGOs) played a vital role in highlighting the broader implications of the digital divide. Organizations like the World Wide Web Foundation and Digital Rights NGO groups illuminated the social and economic impacts of limited connectivity in less affluent regions. Their studies underscored how digital barriers exacerbated existing inequalities, impeding access to education, healthcare, and economic opportunities.

One notable example is Kenya's initiative with the

implementation of digital learning projects, supported by NGOs and tech companies, to ensure that children in remote areas experience an education not handicapped by lack of digital access. Such projects symbolized the rising tide of awareness and activism aimed at equipping communities with the digital tools necessary for socio-economic advancement.

Moreover, projects like the ambitious "Internet for All" initiative by the World Economic Forum further steered efforts toward collective digital inclusivity. This initiative sought to connect over 500 million individuals across regions of Africa, Latin America, and South Asia, creating models of connectivity that were both affordable and sustainable, largely focusing on community-driven approaches.

Interim Analysis: Incorporating Digital Rights into Human Rights Frameworks

As these early movements gained traction, the need to incorporate digital rights into the greater human rights framework became increasingly apparent. Human rights organizations began foregrounding digital rights in their mandates, stressing the intersectionality of rights and the internet's role in enabling fundamental freedoms.

Efforts like those from the United Nations Human Rights Council have further attempted to position internet access within the universal human rights paradigm. The council passed non-binding resolutions recognizing access to the internet as a facilitator of rights outlined in the Universal Declaration of Human Rights, notably freedoms of expression and association.

Notwithstanding these efforts, challenges loom large. Disparities in digital infrastructure, inclusive of gendered technology gaps, affordability issues, and geopolitical tensions over information control, underscore the complex journey toward universal digital rights recognition. These challenges, however, also signify potential areas for future growth and collaboration, bridging the chasms that hinder the fulfillment of a truly interconnected world.

The Case of Rwanda: A Practical Application

While optimism runs high, practical applications remain key to realizing digital rights as a de facto human right. To this end, the case of Rwanda serves as an instructive example. In the mid-2000s, under the Vision 2020 initiative, Rwanda embarked on an ambitious journey to establish itself as a knowledge-based economy. Recognizing broadband access as a critical underpinning, the Rwandan government alongside partners invested heavily in developing nationwide fiber-optic networks.

This strategic investment laid the groundwork for the proliferation of innovative digital solutions, particularly in government services (such as paperless governance models) and educational access. Complemented by supportive policies and partnerships, initiatives like One Laptop per Child further exemplified Rwanda's commitment to bridging the digital divide from the ground up.

Rwanda's narrative distinctly echoes the subchapter's core message: that early recognition, sustained commitment, and collaborative action can transform digital rights from idealistic aspirations into on-the-ground realities. As this evolution persists, so too does the broader question of defining connectivity as the hinge upon which the next chapter of human rights revolves.

Looking forward, as readers move into the forthcoming chapters, they are invited to consider their place in this digital evolution, exploring how interwoven connectivity and rights redefine our collective human experience.

In Chapter 1, "The Evolution of Human Rights," we embarked on a comprehensive exploration of how the very notion of human rights has transformed over centuries. We began by unraveling the philosophical and political origins that laid the groundwork for individual freedoms, tracing their evolution through seminal documents like the Magna Carta and the Declaration of the Rights of Man. This historical foundation set the stage for the global recognition of human rights as essential, with the formation of universal frameworks epitomized by the United Nations and milestones such as the Universal Declaration of Human Rights.

Progressing into the 20th century, the relentless force of social movements further expanded the boundaries of human rights, driving societal change and redefining fundamental rights through collective action in diverse arenas of justice. As we approached our digital age, we faced the dual-edged nature of technology's impact on rights, highlighting new challenges and opportunities in the digital realm. This shift brought about the critical discourse on digital rights, urging us to recognize internet access as a fundamental right and an emerging focal point of human dignity.

As we conclude this examination of human rights evolution, you, the reader, are encouraged to reflect on these transformations and consider the implications in your own professional and personal spheres. The dynamic intersection of technology and human rights beckons us to actively participate in shaping future narratives where connectivity is a universal lifeline.

Looking forward, Chapter 2 will delve deeper into the role of digital rights in our interconnected world, scrutinizing how the principles we've explored continue to evolve. Join us as we navigate this new frontier, exploring how we can harness digital connectivity to further social equity and global empowerment.

CHAPTER 2: PHILOSOPHICAL FOUNDATIONS OF DIGITAL RIGHTS

I n an era defined by the omnipresence of digital connectivity, the very nature of what it means to have rights is undergoing profound transformation. As we navigate this new frontier, it is imperative to explore the philosophical underpinnings that guide our understanding of digital rights. This chapter embarks on a journey into the heart of these philosophies, illuminating the evolving landscape of rights in the digital age. Drawing on the rich tapestry of traditional and modern philosophical thought, we will begin to unravel the complexities of defining and defending digital rights as fundamental to human existence.

To understand the modern discourse of digital rights, we begin with a dissection of traditional rights in their historical context. Subchapter 2.1 lays the vital groundwork, delving into the inherent characteristics of rights and their translation into the digital sphere. Here, we scrutinize the metamorphosis of conventional rights and explore how they forge new pathways into the digital realm. This foundational discussion sets the stage for considering digital rights not as novel inventions but as natural extensions of universally acknowledged human rights.

Building upon this framework, Subchapter 2.2 taps into the existential dimensions of digital rights. Through the lens of existential philosophers such as Jean-Paul Sartre and Simone de Beauvoir, we question the essence of freedom, existence, and identity in the digital era. This section provokes contemplation about the digital world's impact on personal autonomy and agency, challenging us to consider whether digital rights might indeed serve as liberating tools for existential freedom.

The dialogue advances in Subchapter 2.3, where we examine the interaction between digital rights and the public sphere. Influenced by the critical theories of Jürgen Habermas and Hannah Arendt, this segment discusses the transformative power of digital platforms in shaping public discourse and democratic participation. It argues for reconceptualizing internet access as a civil right indispensable to active citizenship in modern democracies.

As we delve deeper, Subchapter 2.4 invites us to contemplate the ethical dimensions of digital rights. In this section, the ethical paradigms of utilitarianism and deontology provide frameworks for investigating the interplay between digital rights and ethical obligations. Here, the chapter confronts pressing challenges related to privacy, surveillance, and data ownership, seeking a harmonious balance between digital advancement and ethical stewardship.

Concluding our exploration, Subchapter 2.5 addresses the ontological impact of digital connectivity on human existence. Through Martin Heidegger's concept of 'Being-in-the-world,' this final section examines how digital rights reshape our fundamental understanding of being and identity. As we dissect the profound effects of digital spaces on human interconnectedness, this discussion serves as a segue into subsequent chapters, which will explore technology's role as a catalyst for humanity's evolution.

Through these philosophical explorations, this chapter invites readers into a deeper understanding of digital rights as a crucial facet of modern human experience. As Dr. Eleanor Rees's articulate narrative guides us through this intricate web of ideas, we are called not only to comprehend but also to engage in the ongoing conversation about our digital future and the rights that underpin it.

Subchapter 2.1: The Conceptual Framework of Rights in the Digital Era

In exploring the philosophical foundations of digital rights, it is essential to first understand what constitutes a "right" in its traditional context. Throughout history, the concept of rights has evolved to encapsulate fundamental principles that govern the relationships between individuals and the state, prescribing both entitlements and duties. At its core, a right is an abstract construct that signifies the freedom to act or refrain from acting, with outcomes often protected or enforced by legal or ethical norms. In Western philosophy, the notion of rights gained substantial momentum during the Enlightenment, with philosophers such as John Locke and Jean-Jacques Rousseau laying the groundwork for modern theories of human rights.

As we transition to the digital age, these traditional activities of assertion, acquisition, and enforcement of rights encounter new challenges and require redefinition against the backdrop of technological advances. The pre-digital understanding of rights is often deeply rooted in tangible experiences, property rights pertain to physical goods, freedom of speech to oral or written expressions, and privacy to personal spaces. However, in a digital context, these abstractions must encompass entities that are intangible, such as data, digital identities, and online interactions. Thus, digital rights emerge as an extension and adaptation of human rights, necessitating a thorough re-engagement with our collective ethical and legislative frameworks.

Intrinsic Characteristics of Rights

Traditionally, rights have intrinsic characteristics that include universality, inalienability, and often, a set of corresponding duties. These attributes ensure that rights are inherently egalitarian, non-transferable, and obligatory within a societal framework. In the digital realm, these characteristics face fresh interpretations. For instance, the universality of internet access, widely advocated as an essential digital right, must address unequal infrastructure deployment and socio-economic disparities that limit its realization on a global scale.

Inalienability, the principle that rights cannot be surrendered or transferred, raises questions in the digital context about consent and ownership. Consider data privacy: individuals frequently "consent" to sharing vast swathes of personal data in exchange for services, raising the question of whether such rights are truly inalienable if they can be ceded so readily, even if under informed consent.

Redefining Rights in the Digital Era

The digital age prompts a necessary redefinition of traditional rights. As technology becomes increasingly pervasive, it challenges the boundaries of personal space, as seen in debates surrounding privacy and data protection. In this landscape, digital rights argue in favor of extending the principle of privacy to digital footprints, mirrored by the need for robust data protection laws like the GDPR in Europe or CCPA in California. These frameworks seek to encode digital privacy as a fundamental right akin to physical privacy, adapting legal structures to safeguard digital expressions and interactions.

Freedom of expression, another cornerstone of traditional rights, similarly evolves within digital contexts. Social media platforms epitomize the modern agora, where ideas are exchanged across borders at unprecedented scale and speed. This evolution necessitates the adaptation of freedom of speech principles to digital dialogues. Debates ensue over content moderation, platform responsibility, and the balance between free expression and misinformation control, reflecting the intricate dynamics within digital rights.

Digital Rights as Human Rights Extensions

Understanding digital rights as extensions of human rights rests upon acknowledging the transformative power technology wields. The internet, as a unifying force, has democratized information access and amplified global voices, proposing a new dimension to equality and freedom. This digital divide, however, underscores the urgency in bridging gaps, ensuring technology serves as a tool for empowerment rather than disenfranchisement, especially for marginalized communities.

To actively integrate digital rights into the framework of human rights, policy architects and legislators worldwide must re-evaluate existing legal frameworks, infusing them with adaptive, forward-thinking measures that accommodate rapid technological change. Such endeavors are paramount not only in developed regions but across the globe, where digital rights hold potential as pivotal instruments of social justice and economic development.

Real-life Case Study: Bridging the Digital Divide

The conceptual intricacies of digital rights can be illustrated through real-life initiatives like Project Loon. Spearheaded by X, the innovation lab within Alphabet Inc., Project Loon sought to address internet accessibility in remote areas by deploying high-altitude balloons to create an aerial wireless network. This endeavor exemplifies bridging the digital divide, highlighting the realization of internet access as a fundamental right.

In regions where traditional infrastructure deployments are economically unfeasible or geographically challenging, initiatives like Project Loon demonstrate the potential of innovative solutions. They not only provide practical applications of digital rights as an extension of human rights but also inspire similar actions across the globe, reinforcing the philosophical arguments that underpin digital rights.

As we continue to redefine rights within the digital domain and explore their real-world impact, the subsequent analysis will delve into how these emerging rights intersect with existential philosophies. We will examine the works of seminal thinkers like Jean-Paul Sartre and Simone de Beauvoir, offering insights into the profound ways in which digital access intertwines with concepts of freedom, existence, and identity.

Subchapter 2.2: Digital Rights in the Context of Existential Philosophy

In the contemporary digital age, the concept of digital rights demands not only a legal and technological perspective but also a profound philosophical discourse. This chapter explores digital rights through the lens of existential philosophy, a field that provides insights into the nature of human freedom, existence, and agency. By examining the works of seminal existential thinkers such as Jean-Paul Sartre and Simone de Beauvoir, this discourse delves into how the digital realm affects our sense of self, autonomy, and the broader quest for meaning.

Existentialism, often associated with the slogan "existence precedes essence," posits that individuals first exist, encounter themselves, and emerge into the world, where they define themselves by their actions and choices. This philosophical outlook sets the stage for a nuanced examination of the digital landscape, where new forms of existence and identity emerge alongside the expansion of digital rights.

Digital Existence and Freedom

Jean-Paul Sartre's notion of freedom emphasizes the absence of predefined essence; individuals must navigate their existence through choices and actions. In the digital world, this translates into a new paradigm of agency and freedom. Digital spaces allow individuals to craft identities, participate in communities, and express themselves beyond geographic constraints. However, with increased freedom comes greater responsibility and new challenges.

For instance, the freedom to express oneself online is tempered by issues of privacy, surveillance, and the digital footprint one leaves behind. The public and private realms blur within social media platforms, raising questions about the extent of freedom and autonomy individuals truly possess. Here, the paradox of choice becomes apparent, digital platforms liberate through choice, yet the overwhelming array of options can lead to decision paralysis or even self-estrangement.

Consider the case of social media influencers who curate online personas that resonate with followers worldwide. The freedom these individuals experience is multifaceted: they possess the power to influence public discourse while simultaneously managing their constructed identities. Yet, the pressure to maintain a consistent image can constrain their actions and decisions, ultimately shaping their existential freedom within a digital context.

Identity and Digital Self-Concept

Simone de Beauvoir extends existentialist thought to include ideas of otherness and the construction of identity. In the digital space, one's sense of self and identity is often mediated through digital interactions. The fluidity of digital identities allows for a multiplicity of selves, challenging the traditional boundaries of identity and self-concept.

Digital rights intersect with identity in profound ways. For marginalized communities, digital spaces can serve as liberating platforms where voices once silenced or marginalized are amplified. Here, digital rights become instruments for asserting one's existence, challenging societal norms, and advocating for equality and justice.

Yet, the digital projection of the self also carries the weight of representation and authenticity. For instance, members of the LGBTQ+ community often find safe havens in digital communities where they can express their identities without fear. The right to digital anonymity can provide safety and freedom, allowing for exploration and acceptance of one's true self. However, the same anonymity can also lead to dehumanization or exploitation, where identity becomes commodified or prejudicially misrepresented.

Agency in the Digital Realm

Existentialist philosophers have long pondered the nature of agency, choice, and personal responsibility. In a digital world, the scope of agency expands dramatically. Digital rights empower individuals to navigate virtual spaces, access information, and engage with the world in unprecedented ways. Yet, they also introduce complex layers of responsibility and ethical consideration.

Consider a young activist using digital platforms to mobilize environmental movements. Armed with the digital right to access information and communicate, they can rapidly spread awareness and galvanize action. However, this empowerment also comes with the responsibility to source credible information and ensure the integrity of online communications.

Moreover, digital agency is influenced by access to digital infrastructures and literacy. The digital divide poses a significant barrier to achieving equal agency globally. While some populations harness the potential of digital spaces, others remain excluded due to lack of access, resources, or education. Digital rights, therefore, must not only encompass the freedom to act but also ensure equitable access to digital tools and resources.

Existential Choices in a Digital Age

The digital landscape offers a fertile ground for existential choices that shape individual destinies and collective futures. With digital rights as a backdrop, individuals are called to contemplate what it means to exist authentically in a virtual world. The decisions made online, whether choosing platforms, creating content, or engaging with communities, reflect wider existential questions about purpose and identity.

A pertinent case study is the rise of digital nomads, individuals who leverage technology to embrace lifestyles untethered from conventional geographic constraints. For them, digital rights such as internet access and freedom of movement become essential to their existential choice of living and working anywhere in the world. Their journeys highlight the interplay between digital freedom, career agency, and the quest for meaning.

As these themes unfold, they underpin the complexity of digital existence in an era where rights are constantly evolving alongside technological advances. The challenge, then, is to cultivate digital spaces that respect and enhance human freedom, identity, and agency, aligning technological progress with existential aspirations.

In the following discussion, we will further explore the

intersection of digital rights with the public sphere, as framed by the philosophies of Jürgen Habermas and Hannah Arendt, continuing our exploration of how digital platforms are reshaping public discourse and democratic participation. This transition invites readers to consider the broader implications of digital rights beyond the individual, into the realms of civic engagement and collective societal transformation.

Subchapter 2.3: Rights, Technology, and the Public Sphere

In the opening chapters of this book, we have examined the traditional and existential philosophical underpinnings of digital rights. Building upon this foundation, we now turn our attention to the role of digital rights within the public sphere, a critical area where rights converge with the collective structures of society and governance. Here, we step beyond individual autonomy to consider the shared spaces where communal discourse and democracy flourish or falter. We draw upon the philosophies of Jürgen Habermas and Hannah Arendt, who provide profound insights into public discourse and democratic participation, concepts increasingly mediated through digital platforms in the modern world.

The Digital Platform as a Public Sphere

The concept of the public sphere, as articulated by Jürgen Habermas, is central to understanding how digital rights operate within societal discourse. According to Habermas, the public sphere is a domain of social life where public opinion can be formed, a space for individuals to come together to discuss and influence political action. The internet has arguably transformed and expanded this sphere, offering nearly limitless potential for participation. Yet, with this expansion comes a labyrinth of challenges: misinformation, digital divides, and the concentration of platform power. Digital rights in this context can be seen as the tools necessary for ensuring equitable access, participation, and representation within these digital realms.

A tangible example of the digital public sphere in action is the Arab Spring. Throughout the early 2010s, social media became a cornerstone for organizing protests and disseminating information among activist groups and individuals challenging oppressive regimes. By leveraging platforms like Facebook and Twitter, ordinary citizens entered a dialogue with national narratives, influencing political landscapes in ways previously unimaginable. The Arab Spring underscores the importance of digital rights such as freedom of expression and access to information for sustaining and nurturing democratic processes.

The Nature of Civic Rights in the Digital Age

With the digital public sphere in focus, we must consider whether access to the internet should be recognized as a civic right. Here, Hannah Arendt's notion of the vita activa, active life, comes to prominence. Arendt emphasizes the importance of action and public participation as fundamental to human existence. In our digital age, the internet acts as a conduit for such interactions, making it as vital to civic life as roads and public squares were in earlier times.

In recognizing the internet as a civic right, we advocate for the instrumentalization of digital platforms as enablers of active citizenship. Consider Estonia, often heralded as a digital nation. Its e-residency program allows citizens to access government services online, vote digitally, and engage in public decision-making processes from anywhere in the world. This model showcases how integrating digital rights within public policy can enhance civic engagement and democratize participation, embodying Arendt's vision of an active, participatory public life.

Challenges: Misinformation and Privacy

Despite their transformative potential, digital spaces pose

significant challenges akin to those Habermas warns against: commercialization of the public sphere and reduction of discourse quality. The internet has become fertile ground for misinformation, threatening to distort public opinion and complicate the exercise of informed citizenship. Platforms, often regulated inconsistently across jurisdictions, grapple with the balance between moderating content and preserving users' rights to free expression.

Moreover, the question of privacy pervades digital discourse. As Arendt cautions, a space dominated by surveillance can stifle authentic participation. The Cambridge Analytica scandal exemplifies the perils of data misuse, where personal information was weaponized for political manipulation, undermining the integrity of democratic processes. Ensuring the sanctity of digital rights, therefore, necessitates robust privacy protections and transparent data practices, empowering citizens to participate without fear of exploitation or surveillance.

Ensuring Equitable Digital Participation

Addressing the digital divide remains a pivotal task in achieving a truly inclusive public sphere. As Habermas emphasizes, a legitimate public domain is one accessible to all, a notion complicated by disparities in digital literacy and internet accessibility. Bridging this divide requires not just policy initiatives but comprehensive educational strategies to empower users with the skills necessary to navigate, critically assess, and actively engage in digital spaces.

Innovative initiatives can be observed across the globe. Take Kenya's M-PESA program, which transformed mobile phones into banking terminals, a development that catalyzed financial inclusion in regions often excluded from traditional banking systems. By harnessing the digital sphere, such initiatives demonstrate the power of technology to bridge gaps and foster greater civic participation across socio-economic barriers.

A Case Study: The Network Society

As we navigate the intersection of digital rights and the public sphere, the concept of a 'network society', as explored by sociologist Manuel Castells, becomes pertinent. A network society is characterized by social structures centered on networks enabled by digital technologies. In Castells' analysis, these structures are highly dynamic, transitioning from traditional forms of community and governance to more fluid, decentralized networks that redefine social relations.

Consider the case of municipal broadband initiatives in the United States. In cities like Chattanooga, Tennessee, local governments have implemented public broadband services to ensure residents can access reliable, high-speed internet. These initiatives not only enhance connectivity but democratize access to the public sphere, empowering citizens to participate fully in the digital economy and in civic life. Chattanooga's success story emphasizes the potential for local governance to foster equitable access, embodying the ideals of the network society.

Ultimately, as we advance through these complex landscapes, the interplay between digital rights, technology, and the public sphere calls for continual reflection. Just as technology evolves, so too must our philosophical, legal, and societal frameworks to ensure that digital rights are preserved and promoted as essential components of citizenship and public life. Moving forward, we will explore the ethical dimensions that underpin these rights, navigating the tensions between technological advancements and moral imperatives that shape our interconnected existence.

Subchapter 2.4: Ethical Dimensions of Digital Rights

The digital landscape is vibrant and rapidly evolving, raising profound ethical questions about the rights of individuals and societies in an interconnected world. When discussing ethical dimensions, we traverse understanding that encompasses complex philosophical inquiries and practical societal implications. Digital rights embody more than just access to technology; they encapsulate our moral obligations and duties towards each other in a digital society. In this subchapter, we will delve deeply into the ethical frameworks of utilitarianism and deontology, as well as other pertinent philosophies, to explore how they guide us in navigating the moral terrain of the digital realm. Furthermore, we shall provide practical examples and case studies to illustrate how these theories apply to questions of privacy, surveillance, data ownership, and more.

Utilitarianism: Maximizing Positive Outcomes

Utilitarianism, a predominant ethical framework proposed by philosophers such as Jeremy Bentham and John Stuart Mill, emphasizes maximizing happiness or utility for the greatest number of people. In the context of digital rights, utilitarianism could guide decisions regarding technology development, data management, and privacy laws. For example, allowing extensive data collection could lead to faster medical research or improved national security, potentially benefiting society as a whole.

Take the scenario of contact tracing apps used during pandemics. These applications require accessing and processing large sets of personal data to track the spread of a virus effectively. Utilitarianism would support the deployment of such technology if it significantly reduces the spread of disease and saves lives. However, this approach raises the ethical dilemma of balancing public health benefits with the individual's right to privacy. While utilitarianism appears straightforward in its intent to maximize collective good, it often sacrifices individual rights, posing challenges in wholly applying it to digital rights scenarios.

Deontology: Duty and Rights

Deontological ethics, primarily associated with Immanuel Kant, prioritizes duties and principles over consequences. In the digital realm, a deontological perspective demands strict adherence to individual rights and moral rules. It emphasizes respect for persons as ends in themselves, not merely as means to an end, underscoring the importance of safeguarding individual digital rights regardless of broader societal benefits.

Consider the issue of data privacy. From a deontological point of view, individuals have an inherent right to control their personal information, and organizations have a duty to protect this data, regardless of potential advantages in aggregating user data for broader applications. A deontological approach to digital rights upholds that privacy laws are non-negotiable moral imperatives.

A practical illustration of deontological principles can be seen in the European Union's General Data Protection Regulation (GDPR), which enshrines the fundamental right of individuals to privacy and data protection, compelling companies to ensure stringent data handling practices. This rigid adherence to privacy rights showcases a deontological commitment often conflicting with utilitarian motives for data usage.

Balancing Digital Advancement with Ethical Responsibilities

The challenge lies in balancing technological advancements with a commitment to ethical responsibility. This balance demands a nuanced understanding that neither utilitarian nor deontological frameworks alone can sufficiently address the complexities of digital rights; rather, they must be integrated and applied contextually.

One effort to balance these ethical stances can be observed in the implementation of ethical AI guidelines. Many organizations and governments are now advocating for AI systems that are both beneficial to society and respectful of individual rights. Such guidelines often derive from a synthesis of utilitarian goals with deontological protections, aiming to foster innovation while safeguarding fundamental human rights.

Privacy, Surveillance, and Data Ownership

Modern challenges in digital rights, such as privacy, surveillance, and data ownership, illustrate the intricate balance between individual freedoms and collective benefits.

1. Privacy: In an era of ubiquitous connectivity and constant data flow, privacy has become a pivotal ethical issue. Privacy is not merely about keeping information secret; it involves control over personal boundaries in the digital sphere. Ethical considerations must weigh the individual's right to privacy against social benefits derived from data collection and sharing.

2. Surveillance: The potential for surveillance in digital spaces raises ethical questions regarding autonomy and freedom. In a surveillance-oriented digital environment, individuals may feel compelled to self-censor, impacting freedom of expression, a fundamental right in democratic societies. The balance lies in ethically justifying surveillance practices without infringing on individual rights to freedom.

3. Data Ownership: As information becomes an invaluable asset, debates over data ownership highlight the clash between utilitarian benefits of shared data and individual rights to data control. Who truly owns your digital footprint, the individual or the corporation collecting it? The ethical responsibility demands ensuring that individuals maintain control over their own data, respecting their autonomy and privacy.

Case Study: The Facebook-Cambridge Analytica Scandal

The infamous Facebook-Cambridge Analytica scandal serves as a poignant case study for examining ethical dilemmas in digital rights. In 2018, it was revealed that Cambridge Analytica harvested data of millions of Facebook users without consent, using it for political advertising. This breach of trust ignited global outrage, highlighting ethical transgressions related to privacy invasion and unauthorized data usage.

From a utilitarian perspective, one might argue that the data was employed in a manner that could potentially serve democratic processes through targeted campaigning. However, the lack of informed consent from individuals constitutes a grave ethical violation under deontological principles. The scandal also underscored the need for robust data protection laws and ethical standards, prompting global policies to safeguard digital rights.

Towards an Ethical Digital Future

As we transition from ethical discussions to practical applications, it becomes imperative to envision a digital future where rights are both protected and enhanced. It involves creating frameworks where technology innovation aligns with ethical tenets to create equitable digital societies.

Each individual and organization must assume responsibility for upholding ethical digital practices, ensuring that technology serves as a catalyst for empowerment rather than exploitation. This digital ethics dialogue will continue to evolve, guiding us toward cohesive strategies that reconcile innovation with rights and duties.

Such discussions naturally pave the way for further exploration of how interconnectedness and technology influence human existence. As we conclude this subchapter, we turn our focus to the ontological impact of digital connectivity, examining its implications on our understanding of being and existence in an increasingly digital world. Through examining ethics, ontology, and philosophy together, we gain a comprehensive insight into the philosophy of digital rights, interweaving our understanding of ethics with the broader digital life fabric that defines our age.

Subchapter 2.5: The Ontological Impact of Digital Connectivity

As we delve into the ontological implications of digital connectivity, we find ourselves at the confluence of technology and the human experience. Ontology, the philosophical study of being, is a lens through which we can explore how digital rights influence our understanding of existence. The application of digital rights is not simply a matter of policy or regulation; it is an exploration of the lived human condition in a world increasingly mediated by digital interfaces.

We must begin by examining Martin Heidegger's notion of 'Being-in-the-world,' which provides a backdrop for understanding how digital spaces have fundamentally reshaped our conception of self and existence. In our traditional, physical existence, 'Being-in-the-world' referred to the intrinsic relationship between humans and their environment, how individuals exist in relation to the world around them. However, with the advent of digital connectivity, this relationship has undergone a seismic shift, merging the digital and physical into a hybrid space of existence.

For instance, consider the way social media platforms redefine notions of presence and absence. On platforms like Facebook or Twitter, a person's digital presence can be constant and highly interactive, even when they are physically absent. This digital presence challenges traditional notions of space and time, suggesting an existence that transcends physical boundaries. Our 'digital selves' become essential aspects of our identity, avatars that coexist with our physical forms.

Moreover, digital connectivity has introduced new dimensions of identity formation. In the digital world, anonymity can allow individuals to explore various facets of their identity without the constraints imposed by societal norms. This freedom to experiment can lead to greater self-discovery and acceptance, but it can also compel individuals to question the authenticity and permanence of their identities. Anonymity provides space for expression but may also obscure accountability and genuine engagement.

Consider the profound impact of digital rights on personal freedom and autonomy. Access to digital information and communication tools empowers individuals to learn, express themselves, and take part in global conversations. However, this same connectivity exposes individuals to new vulnerabilities. In countries with limited digital rights, censorship and state surveillance stifle expression, limiting the ability of individuals to fully express their agency. This dichotomy underscores the necessity of attaching ontological importance to digital rights and access.

To illustrate, let's examine a real-world example: the 2010 Arab Spring. Digital connectivity played a crucial role in organizing protests and sharing information across North Africa and the Middle East. Social media platforms served as catalysts for democracy, empowering citizens to voice their dissent and challenge oppressive regimes. Individuals who participated in these movements inhabited digital spaces as forums for activism, creating online communities that rallied support and solidarity. The virtual existence enabled by digital rights directly influenced the physical realm, demonstrating the interconnectedness of digital and physical being.

On a more personal level, technology's encroachment into everyday life begs us to consider how digital rights influence the intimate relationships individuals have with their own existence. Heidegger's notion of authenticity, living in a way true to one's own beliefs and values, is challenged in digital societies where curated online personas might overshadow genuine expressions of self. Digital rights, if poorly implemented, can contribute to a culture of surveillance capitalism, where privacy is sacrificed for convenience, and algorithmic control shapes human behavior in unseen ways.

As an example, consider the case of data privacy and its ontological implications. As technology evolves, individuals are often unaware of the extent to which their personal data is harvested, analyzed, and sold. This commodification of personal information can lead to an erosion of individual autonomy and a reshaping of personal identity based on algorithmically curated suggestions. Such practices prompt a reexamination of digital rights' role in protecting the sanctity of selfhood and ensuring that individuals maintain control over their digital likeness.

Let's take a look at a hypothetical example to better understand these concepts. Imagine a world where virtual reality (VR) becomes the dominant medium for social interaction. People work, learn, and socialize primarily in immersive virtual environments, blurring the lines between digital and physical existence. In this world, digital rights such as access to VR technology, privacy protection, and data ownership become paramount for individual autonomy. Without strong digital rights, users might be subjected to manipulation by corporations that control the virtual realms, with the power to alter perceptions and behaviors without users' knowledge.

For individuals in this world, 'Being-in-the-world' would require navigating both the digital and physical landscapes with equal importance. Personal identity might be redefined with every interaction in virtual spaces, necessitating new frameworks for understanding relationships and communities. Questions around authenticity, agency, and freedom become ever more pressing.

In summation, the ontological impact of digital connectivity cannot be understated. It challenges our foundational understandings of existence and identity, reshaping how we interact with the world and each other. A robust framework for digital rights is essential to protect these dimensions of human experience, ensuring that technology serves as a bridge to greater freedom and self-discovery rather than a barrier. As we transition toward the final discussions of this chapter and beyond, it is imperative to continue examining how digital rights can encapsulate and promote the true essence of humanity in an increasingly digital age.

We now move towards practical applications of these philosophical insights, which will help illuminate their significance in everyday contexts. Consider the education sector, where digital connectivity has a pronounced ontological impact on both students' and teachers' experiences. In digital classrooms, remote learning technologies connect students across geographical boundaries, democratizing access to information and enabling diverse learning communities. However, the quality of digital access, ensured by digital rights, can dictate the effectiveness and equity of these learning environments.

In one case study from an NGO working in rural India, schools that integrated digital connectivity into their curriculums saw a marked increase in participation and overall educational outcomes. Students could engage with rich digital content unavailable in traditional settings, accessing lectures by leading academics worldwide. However, these benefits were only realized due to the concerted effort to establish robust digital connections and advocate for students' rights to access and privacy. This effort underscores the centrality of digital rights in transforming educational landscapes, promoting inclusivity, and fostering a sense of belonging for all students, key components of their ontological being.

Therefore, as educators, policy-makers, and citizens, recognizing the ontological dimensions of digital rights is fundamental. The digital revolution offers both opportunities and challenges in redefining human existence. Our continuous examination of these philosophical foundations is essential, not only for understanding but also for actively shaping a digital age that honors and expands the full scope of human potential.

As we navigate the philosophical landscape of digital rights, Chapter 2 has unearthed the layered complexities that underpin this modern extension of human rights. We began by unpacking the foundational concept of 'rights,' transitioning from traditional understandings to their evolving interpretations in our digital age. This shift underscores the importance of recognizing digital rights as not merely ancillary but central to the dialogues surrounding human dignity and freedom.

In our exploration of existential philosophy, we drew on the writings of thinkers like Sartre and de Beauvoir, probing how digital access fundamentally shapes individual autonomy and identity. This inquiry revealed digital rights as potential enablers of existential freedom, emphasizing the profound implications of digital connectivity on personal agency.

Our journey then advanced to the public sphere, where the philosophies of Habermas and Arendt informed our understanding of internet access as an essential civic right. In this digital epoch, such access not only reshapes democratic participation but becomes a linchpin of active citizenship, highlighting the internet's transformational potential in public discourse.

We also grappled with the ethical dimensions of digital rights, recognizing that balancing these with ethical duties is paramount. By confronting issues such as privacy and surveillance, we affirmed the need to ethically steward the digital realm while bolstering individual rights.

Concluding with the ontological impact of digital connectivity, we marveled at how digital rights influence our very sense of being. Here, Heidegger's notion of 'Being-in-the-world' served as a philosophical beacon, illuminating how interconnectedness redefines identity and human experience.

As we pivot to the next chapter, we carry forward these foundational insights to examine technology as humanity's transformative catalyst. Let us venture forward, armed with a deeper understanding and inspired to weave these philosophical insights into practice within our interconnected world.

CHAPTER 3: TECHNOLOGY AS HUMANITY'S CATALYST

As we journey into Chapter 3 of Connected Rights: Reimagining Human Freedom in the Digital Age, we find ourselves at the intriguing intersection of technology and humanity, a crossroad where modern innovations serve as the catalyst for reshaping the scope of human freedom. In this chapter, Dr. Eleanor Rees invites us to reconsider what it means to wield technology as a tool for personal and collective empowerment in an increasingly digital world.

Set against a backdrop of historical and philosophical reflections from earlier sections, this chapter delves into the nuances of technology's dual capacity to both liberate and constrain. Through meticulously crafted narratives, Dr. Rees unravels the complexities of our digital dependencies, urging us to contemplate the profound implications they hold for human rights today.

The discussion opens with an exploration of the ambivalent nature of digital tools. Here, we confront their paradoxical role as both nurturers of expression and potential suppressors of autonomy, posing significant questions about our digital engagements. Dr. Rees rigorously examines this duality, laying the groundwork for understanding the intricate dance between technology and agency.

Progressing from this duality, the narrative transitions into a reflection on how digital platforms are revolutionizing social interactions and community dynamics. Through her insightful lens, Dr. Rees uncovers how these virtual spaces break down long-standing social barriers, fostering greater inclusivity and participation. This examination reveals a transformation of societal hierarchies, enhancing the dialogue on how digital landscapes can redefine human rights engagement.

In the age of algorithms, a critical chapter awaits as Dr. Rees pivots to examine their profound influence on our lives. From shaping personal decisions to curating the information we consume, algorithms are ever-present, and their impacts are both illuminating and daunting. This section of the chapter implores us to engage in a crucial conversation about preserving agency amidst machine-driven environments.

As the digital train rolls forward, the chapter shifts focus to the digital divide's harsh reality. Here, the narrative tackles disparities in technology access, underscoring the necessity for equitable digital resource distribution. The analysis provides a somber reflection on how this divide impedes personal freedom and community advancement, setting the stage for deeper exploration of digital equity in subsequent discussions.

The chapter culminates with riveting case studies that spotlight pioneers of digital empowerment. These narratives are not merely tales of adversity overcome but are vivid demonstrations of technology's potential when harnessed purposefully to ignite social change. Dr. Rees uses these stories to inspire a powerful vision of what digital empowerment can achieve, leaving us with a sense of optimism and anticipation for the ethical and legal frameworks to be discussed ahead.

Chapter 3 stands as a pivotal point in the book, bridging theoretical insights with tangible illustrations of technology's impact on human freedom. These diverse explorations invite readers to critically engage with technology's role as a catalyst, preparing them for the nuanced discussions that lie ahead. Through Dr. Rees's expert storytelling, we are called to reflect, question, and potentially transform our digital futures.

Subchapter 3.1: The Dual Edge of Digital Tools

In a world increasingly interconnected through digital platforms and technologies, the line between empowerment and restriction grows ever more complex and nuanced. Dr. Eleanor Rees delves into this critical paradigm, where on one hand technology acts as a liberating force, yet on the other, it possesses the potential to constrain and even intrude upon our personal freedoms. This dual-edged nature of digital tools forms a significant part of the broader narrative of technology as a catalyst for human progress.

To comprehend the dichotomous impact of digital technology, it is imperative to first explore how digital tools serve as enhancers of human agency. Consider the advent of social media platforms, which have democratized access to information and provided unprecedented channels for communication. A simple smartphone, connected to the internet, empowers individuals with the tools to start movements, educate themselves, and engage with communities across the globe. However, the very same platforms that enable free expression can also become mechanisms of restriction and control.

A poignant example of digital empowerment is the Arab Spring, a series of anti-government protests and uprisings across the Arab world during the early 2010s. Digital platforms, particularly social media, played a pivotal role in these movements by allowing citizens to organize protests, share information with the international community, and shape the narratives of their struggles. These tools acted as agents of empowerment, amplifying voices that would otherwise remain unheard.

Equally notable is the role of digital technology in empowering marginalized groups. The Global Digital Divide: Bridging the Last Frontier by Dr. Rees herself provides numerous case studies where individuals in remote or underserved regions have harnessed technology to break through traditional socioeconomic barriers. For women and minorities in many parts of the world, the internet can be a lifeline to education, financial independence, and political participation. Crowdsourcing platforms, for example, have enabled female entrepreneurs in regions with limited access to financial institutions to launch businesses and sustain livelihoods.

Yet, with the boon of digital technology also comes the bane of surveillance and data manipulation. The same social media that gave rise to the Arab Spring has also become a tool for authoritarian regimes to surveil, control, and manipulate public opinion. Governments and private corporations alike have access to sophisticated surveillance technologies, enabling them to monitor communications, track movements, and even predict behaviors through data analytics.

The Cambridge Analytica scandal is a case in point, illustrating how personal data harvested from social media platforms was used to sway political outcomes. Millions of users had their data unknowingly manipulated to influence opinions and behavior on massive scales. Such incidents underscore the vulnerability of digital tools when wielded with intentions that contrast their liberating potential.

In a digital ecosystem teeming with information, the manipulation of data extends beyond surveillance. It affects autonomy over personal narratives and influences decision-making processes. Algorithms, often designed to maximize engagement and profit, may unfairly shape exposure to information, reinforcing biases and limiting diverse perspectives. The echo chamber effect, where individuals are exposed primarily to information that aligns with their existing beliefs, can restrict cognitive freedom and hinder pluralistic discourse.

In recognizing the dual edge of digital tools, education and critical digital literacy emerge as vital components in navigating this complex terrain. Users must be equipped with the skills to scrutinize the sources and intentions behind digital content, ensuring that technology enhances rather than restricts their agency. Educational initiatives, like those launched by organizations promoting internet literacy in disadvantaged regions, demonstrate how awareness and understanding can empower individuals to make informed choices in the digital realm.

Take the initiative by Mozilla's Web Literacy Project, an international effort to promote digital skills worldwide. This project provides an exemplary model of how enhancing digital literacy can fundamentally alter the balance of empowerment and restriction. By educating users on privacy settings, responsible online behavior, and critical analysis of content, the Web Literacy Project helps shift the agency back to individuals, allowing them to harness technology to improve their lives rather than being passively shaped by it.

Similarly, collaborative projects like the Digital India campaign strive to provide technology access and literacy to rural and underserved communities in India. By facilitating digital infrastructure and awareness, these initiatives aim to empower citizens to harness digital tools effectively and responsibly. This creates a fabric of digitally literate individuals capable of counteracting the restrictive potential of technology.

Through these real-world applications, Dr. Rees underscores the fundamental need for a balanced approach towards digital tools that recognizes their power as both enhancers and potential inhibitors of human freedom. By fostering critical engagement and informed use, society can navigate the paradox of digital empowerment, ensuring that technology fulfills its promise as a true catalyst for human advancement.

This exploration of the dual edge of digital tools sets the stage for understanding broader societal transformations driven by technology. As we transition to the next subchapter, the focus shifts to reimagining social dynamics and unraveling how interconnected networks redefine human interaction, influence, and participation across diverse communities. Through this lens, we continue to explore how the digital age reshapes the core tenets of human freedom and social equity.

Subchapter 3.2: Reimagining Social Dynamics

In the digital age, technology has irrevocably transformed the landscape of human interaction, reimagining social dynamics in both unforeseen and profound ways. Dr. Eleanor Rees meticulously examines this transformation, guiding readers through the complex interplay between digital technologies and societal structures. She brings to light the emergence of virtual networks that defy geographic and cultural boundaries to create new avenues for dialogue, participation, and community building. This subchapter embarks on a journey to unravel how technology is not just a medium for communication, but a force that is reshaping the very fabric of human relationships and societal engagement.

Digital Communities: Breaking Down Barriers

Technology has ushered in an era where digital communities seamlessly transcend traditional societal borders, offering a level of inclusivity previously unattainable. These communities have created environments where individuals can unite based on shared interests, goals, or problems, often irrespective of geographic location. Through social media platforms, forums, and virtual communities, people from diverse backgrounds can now engage in conversations and initiatives that span continents.

Dr. Rees highlights platforms like Reddit and Facebook Groups as modern agorae. On Reddit, for example, niche communities known as subreddits offer spaces for dialogue that range from highly technical topics to supportive environments for mental health. These platforms encourage open and dynamic conversation, providing voices to those who may be marginalized in offline spaces. Such digital environments also facilitate the sharing of diverse perspectives, encouraging broader understanding and empathy among participants.

The Role of Technology in Fostering Inclusivity

As digital platforms become more pervasive, they also serve as powerful tools for fostering inclusivity. These spaces cater to issues of accessibility and representation, giving marginalized communities a platform to advocate for their rights. For instance, platforms like Twitter have become vital spaces for social movements, as seen in hashtags such as MeToo and BlackLivesMatter. They allow for rapid dissemination of information and can galvanize global support and action.

These movements illustrate that digital spaces not only amplify marginalized voices but also facilitate the organization of collective action. In countries with oppressive regimes, encrypted messaging apps like Signal and Telegram have enabled activists to coordinate protests safely and effectively. By breaking down barriers to participation, technology empowers individuals and communities to challenge the status quo and seek equitable treatment.

Shifting Power Dynamics in the Digital Sphere

The digital environment also impacts traditional hierarchies within societal structures. In industries such as journalism, where news was once dominated by large media corporations, citizen journalism now offers alternative perspectives and an expansion of voices contributing to public discourse. Platforms like YouTube and Medium allow individuals to publish content with minimal barriers, challenging legacy media establishments and democratizing information access.

Moreover, crowdfunding platforms such as Patreon and Kickstarter harness the power of collective financial support to empower creators and entrepreneurs who might otherwise lack access to traditional funding avenues. By decentralizing influence over cultural production and business development, these platforms disrupt conventional power dynamics, fostering an era of grassroots innovation.

Case Study: The Evolution of Wikipedia

Wikipedia stands as a quintessential example of how technological platforms can alter social structures and democratize knowledge creation and distribution. Founded in 2001 as an open-collaborative platform, Wikipedia invites anyone with internet access to contribute and edit content. This model revolutionizes the traditional flow of information, transferring the role of gatekeepers from a select few to a global community of users.

The platform encapsulates the potential for collective

intelligence to create a comprehensive and diverse knowledge base. Wikipedia is not without its challenges, including debates over accuracy and biases, yet it remains a testament to how digital platforms can harness communal efforts to construct globally accessible resources.

Challenges and Critiques of Digital Social Dynamics

While digital technologies hold incredible potential for inclusivity and participation, they are not without challenges. The very mechanisms that facilitate open communication can also enable the spread of misinformation and create echo chambers that reinforce existing biases. Algorithms guiding social media feeds might prioritize engagement over balanced perspectives, leading to polarization.

Trolling and digital harassment present very real threats to the safety and well-being of individuals in online environments. These challenges underscore the importance of cultivating digital literacy and ethical frameworks that advocate for respectful and constructive online interactions.

Ensuring Ethical Practices in Digital Communities

Ethical concerns surrounding the use of digital technologies are paramount. Dr. Rees emphasizes the responsibility of both platform developers and users to promote environments conducive to constructive engagement. Platform policies must keep pace with evolving technology, ensuring they protect users from abuse while maintaining avenues for free expression.

Educational efforts to foster digital literacy are critical; they empower individuals to critically assess information sources and engage positively in digital discourse. Schools and organizations play vital roles in developing curricula that address these issues, equipping individuals with the tools needed to navigate the digital landscape responsibly.

Practical Application: Building Inclusive Digital Communities

To illustrate the principles discussed, we explore the story of the OpenIDEO platform. Originally established to leverage collective creativity to tackle social issues, OpenIDEO invites individuals worldwide to co-create solutions through design thinking challenges. These challenges cover a broad spectrum, from combating climate change to enhancing childhood education.

Through OpenIDEO, participants collaborate across sectors and geographies, exchanging insights and expertise to develop actionable solutions. The platform's success in cultivating an active community demonstrates the potential for digital spaces to function as crucibles for innovation and social impact.

Participants' diverse backgrounds contribute to a richness of ideas, breaking down preconceived notions of exclusivity in problem-solving. OpenIDEO embodies how technology, when harnessed effectively, can serve as a catalyst for bringing disparate voices together to address global challenges.

As we transition into the discussions of algorithmic influence in the next subchapter, it becomes crucial to consider how these reshaped social dynamics intertwine with technologies like artificial intelligence. These technologies are further redefining our interactions, and the interdependencies between digital engagement and algorithmic governance merit closer examination.

Subchapter 3.3: Agency in the Age of Algorithms

In the contemporary digital world where algorithms increasingly shape the context in which we operate, it's paramount to evaluate their influence on human agency comprehensively. Dr. Eleanor Rees invites us into this exploration with her signature narrative approach, blending academic rigor with relatable insights. Algorithms and artificial intelligence (AI) have revolutionized how we make decisions, access information, and even perceive our capabilities. Yet, understanding their impact isn't merely a scholarly exercise; it's a fundamental necessity for navigating today's algorithm-driven landscapes.

Algorithms dictate which headlines reach the top of our newsfeeds, suggest new music, decide on creditworthiness, customize advertisements, and even influence legal decisions. They are initiated by human programmers, yet they grow, learn, and adapt in ways that can sometimes slip out of their creators' grasp. While their potential for tailoring enhancements is undeniable, Dr. Rees emphasizes a crucial inquiry: amid such automation, how do we sustain or reconstruct individual and collective agency?

The Algorithmic Ecosystem: Opportunity and Control

Algorithms operate based on historical data, learning patterns to predict and deliver everything from movie recommendations on streaming platforms to complex medical diagnoses. This capacity presents enormous opportunities. In health care, for instance, algorithms analyze massive datasets to discover treatment efficacy at unprecedented scales, resulting in life-saving insights. In finance, they can review thousands of transactions per second, detecting potential fraud that human oversight might miss.

However, with opportunities come distinct challenges, particularly regarding privacy and autonomy. One notable concern is the "black box" nature of many AI systems. Decisions may be rendered without insights into how conclusions were reached, inhibiting users' ability to understand or question the results. This opacity can compromise personal agency and autonomy, especially as individuals may unwittingly conform to narratives or decisions generated without their explicit involvement.

Navigating Algorithmic Bias

A significant area within this domain is algorithmic bias. Dr. Rees delves into how, when fueled by incomplete, skewed, or biased datasets, algorithms can perpetuate or even exacerbate existing societal inequalities. For example, consider recidivism prediction algorithms used in the criminal justice system. If the data fed into these systems over-represent particular demographic groups as high risk, the results will likely reinforce those biases, leading to unfair sentencing and systemic injustices.

Conversely, algorithms also have the potential to expose biases rather than entrench them. When properly vetted and ethically deployed, they can offer more consistent and objective decision-making than human arbitrariness, addressing disparities by leveling fields dictated by subjective human flaws.

Transparency and Ethical Algorithm Design

Transparency is a foundational element for ensuring accountability in algorithmic systems. Dr. Rees argues for open-source designs and thorough documentation to render algorithmic processes understandable and auditable. When corporations and developers commit to transparency, it creates pathways for evaluation and improvement, allowing external experts to identify malfunctions, biases, and potential misuses.

Ethical considerations should begin well before an algorithm's deployment. During design and development phases, a concerted effort to include diverse perspectives can mitigate exclusions and disadvantageous outputs. Human-centric views remain vital in finalizing systems intended to aggregate or analyze human preferences, behavior, and reactions.

Exercising Agency: The Human-Algo Partnership

With a deluge of tailored suggestions, humans face the

challenge of determining how much they want to engage with, follow, or reject these insights. Exercising agency in collaboration with algorithms requires a conscious effort: deciding when these systems' counsel adds genuine value and when it limits or misguides.

Take, for instance, personalized learning platforms in education. Students are often presented with material suited to their pace and understanding using algorithmic guidance. However, cultivating critical thinking skills mandates that students occasionally step outside the algorithmically designated paths, exploring diverse content free from algorithm-imposed constraints. The balance between guided progress and independent exploration becomes a matter of agency in navigating educational pathways.

The Road Ahead: Building Ethical Algorithmic Systems

Consider Estonia's transformation from the late 1990s to today as a nation at the forefront of digital governance. It utilizes algorithms across multiple civic services, from voting procedures to tax filings. Remarkably, its e-Residency program enables global entrepreneurs to establish businesses within Estonia's digital realm, facilitated by algorithmic precision and efficiency. This demonstrates the potential of fair, transparent, and empowering algorithmic deployment that respects users' agency while fostering innovation.

The discussions around algorithms traverses both ethical quandaries and real-world applications, each calling for careful consideration. As both citizens and creators within the digital landscape, our grasp of these systems' implications on agency can revolutionize how society harnesses them responsibly. This understanding is paramount as we delve deeper into discussions surrounding technology's equity and its increasingly pivotal role in all aspects of human existence. The forthcoming examination in Subchapter 3.4 addresses another crucial dimension, surmounting the technological divide so that all may equally partake in these digital advancements.

Subchapter 3.4: Bridging the Technological Divide

In our rapidly advancing digital world, access to technology has become as fundamental as access to clean water or education. Yet, the reality of global technological access remains deeply unequal, creating a chasm that persists between various socio-economic and geographical demographics. In this subchapter, Dr. Eleanor Rees delves into the complexities of bridging the technological divide, offering an in-depth analysis of the current state of digital disparity and the ongoing efforts to foster a more equitable digital ecosystem.

Understanding the Divide

The term "technological divide" describes the gap between those with immediate, effective access to digital and information technologies and those without. This divide manifests not only between countries but also within communities, where factors such as income, location, and infrastructure determine one's digital capabilities. Individuals in urban areas of developed countries often take high-speed internet and sophisticated devices for granted. In contrast, their counterparts in rural or underserved regions frequently struggle with basic connectivity, if they have any access at all.

Dr. Rees illustrates this divide through a stark comparison: Consider a student in a bustling city like New York. Armed with a laptop and fast internet, this student can easily access vast educational resources, participate in virtual classroom discussions, and engage with global communities. On the other hand, a student in a rural part of sub-Saharan Africa might have no option but to walk miles to the closest internet café, where outdated and slow computers restrict their learning potential. This disparity extends beyond education, affecting employment opportunities, access to government services, health information, and even social connections.

The Impact of the Divide

The technological divide not only highlights inequities in access but also amplifies broader societal disparities. It perpetuates cycles of poverty and limits socio-economic mobility, ultimately impacting national growth and global development. Communities without robust technological infrastructure are less attractive to potential investors and businesses, which prefer environments with secure digital infrastructures. Lack of access to digital platforms undermines democratic participation, as citizens become unable to voice concerns, mobilize social change, or access crucial information relevant to political processes.

Moreover, the digital divide affects well-being and safety. During the COVID-19 pandemic, for instance, the internet became a lifeline for information on health safety protocols and vaccination. Those without access to digital technology were left isolated, unable to receive critical health updates or telehealth services, further exacerbating health inequalities.

Efforts to Bridge the Gap

Addressing the digital divide requires a multi-faceted approach that involves governments, non-governmental organizations, tech companies, and communities themselves. Several initiatives are setting precedents for practical solutions, illustrating the potential for global and local collaborations to create significant change.

Governments worldwide are pivotal in constructing the policy framework needed for digital inclusivity. Investments in broadband infrastructure, particularly in rural and underserved regions, have shown promising results. South Korea, a leading example, implemented the Broadband Convergence Network program, expanding high-speed internet access to the more isolated and sparsely populated areas of the nation. Similarly, the Indian government's Digital India initiative aims to enhance internet accessibility, providing affordable digital services to rural inhabitants.

Non-governmental organizations play a critical role in complementing governmental efforts. The One Laptop Per Child project seeks to empower children in developing countries by equipping them with specially designed, rugged, and affordable laptops. By focusing on youth, such initiatives ensure that the next generation grows up as competent and confident digital citizens.

Furthermore, tech companies have recognized the moral and economic incentives to participate in bridging the technological divide. Companies like Google and Facebook have experimented with high-altitude balloons and solar-powered drones to provide internet access to remote areas. Satellite internet services are also gaining momentum as viable means to connect communities currently beyond the reach of traditional network infrastructures.

A Case Study: Kenya's Digital Leap

To illustrate the tangible impact of bridging the technological divide, Dr. Rees presents the case study of Kenya, a country that has achieved remarkable progress in expanding digital access. The Kenyan government's collaboration with private entities initiated projects that integrated mobile technology into everyday life. One of the most notable outcomes has been M-Pesa, a mobile money service launched by Safaricom and Vodafone, which revolutionized financial transactions.

Before M-Pesa, a significant portion of Kenya's population remained unbanked, unable to access traditional financial services. The availability of mobile banking allowed users to transfer money, pay bills, and receive salaries via mobile phones, even without a bank account. This innovation not only brought financial services to remote areas but also spurred local economies by facilitating entrepreneurship, particularly among women, thereby narrowing the economic gap.

In terms of education, Kenya's Digital Literacy Programme aimed at providing digital devices to primary school students nationwide, bolstering educational engagement and proficiency. Such efforts have demonstrated that bridging the technological divide is achievable through targeted initiatives, significantly enhancing societal development.

However, challenges remain. Connectivity must be reliable and affordable to ensure long-term success. Comprehensive digital literacy programs are necessary to empower users to take full advantage of the technology at their disposal. Local content creation, relevant and accessible in the native language, further strengthens digital participation by tying global technology advancements to local contexts.

Practical Application: Empowering Women Through Technology

A practical application that reinforces the subchapter's key takeaway is the empowerment of women via digital tools in developing regions. Women in many communities are disproportionately affected by the digital divide due to social and economic barriers. Programs like the UN Women's "WeLearn," an innovative online platform, cater explicitly to women's digital education and skills training.

By providing courses ranging from financial literacy to coding, WeLearn enables women to pursue careers in tech, become entrepreneurs, and participate more actively in community decision-making. The platform conducts sessions in multiple languages, ensuring accessibility and relevance. With Internet connectivity now available in more regions, women armed with digital skills can bridge the gender gap, attaining greater economic independence and social agency.

As we transition to the next subchapter, the spotlight shifts to those pioneering digital empowerment, a theme that resonates with the transformative potential showcased here and further illuminates the diverse narratives of individuals and communities navigating our interconnected world.

Subchapter 3.5: Pioneering Digital Empowerment

As we conclude this multifaceted exploration of technology as humanity's catalyst, it becomes evident that digital empowerment stands as a transformative pillar in the modern age. Dr. Eleanor Rees, in her characteristic style of blending analytical depth with engaging narratives, introduces us to a vivid tapestry of lives reshaped by the judicious use of technology. This subchapter spotlights individuals and communities that are not just surviving but thriving at the intersection of innovation and adversity. With this, we challenge the reader to consider technology as not a mere tool, but as a vehicle of profound human empowerment.

In the 21st century, digital empowerment unfolds in layers, cutting across geographies, cultures, and socio-economic strata. At the heart of this empowerment is the ability to access and leverage digital platforms to foster human rights, community development, and personal growth. This subchapter, through a series of dynamic case studies, underscores the narrative that technology can serve as a catalyst in liberating human potential when consciously harnessed.

Understanding the Foundation of Digital Empowerment

The essence of digital empowerment lies in the availability of resources and knowledge that enable individuals and communities to effect change. This journey begins with ensuring access to foundational digital resources such as internet connectivity, hardware, and software. However, access alone isn't the full picture. True empowerment demands that individuals possess the digital literacy necessary to navigate these resources effectively, transforming potential into real-world impact.

Dr. Rees introduces us to Mariam Diallo from Dakar, Senegal, a poignant example of how digital tools can cross cultural and economic barriers. Mariam, a young entrepreneur, utilized online platforms to launch a thriving business selling eco-friendly products. Her story illustrates how the internet can transcend traditional market limitations, enabling local innovation to ripple out onto a global scale. By leveraging social media for marketing and conducting workshops through video conferencing, Mariam crafted her own path to success, demonstrating the interconnectedness of access, literacy, and empowerment.

Empowerment through Education: The Role of E-learning

The historical barriers to education, limited geographic access, high costs, and resource scarcity, are being dismantled through e-learning platforms. This revolution in education democratizes knowledge, providing expansive opportunities for learning and skill enhancement at an unprecedented scale.

Consider the case of Rajesh Kumar in rural India, who, through online courses, mastered computer programming skills. Despite residing in an area traditionally cut off from high-quality educational resources, Rajesh was able to secure a remote job with an international tech firm. His story is emblematic of the shift towards digital empowerment where geographical location no longer dictates educational opportunities. E-learning platforms empower individuals not only to enhance personal growth but also to contribute more meaningively to their communities, thereby multiplying the impact of access.

Innovative Social Solutions: Community-Led Tech Initiatives

While individual empowerment is crucial, community-driven initiatives hold the potential to enact systemic change. Across the world, collective efforts are harnessing technology to address local challenges, transformative endeavors that embody the spirit of digital empowerment.

In the Philippines, the Banaue Rice Terraces, a UNESCO heritage site, faced degradation due to a lack of awareness and resources. A group of tech-savvy volunteers launched an online campaign combining drones, satellite imagery, and social media to monitor the terraces and raise funds for their preservation. This grassroots initiative not only engaged the global community but also instilled a sense of pride and responsibility among the locals. By illustrating the power of technology to galvanize collective action, this case exemplifies how community-led initiatives can leverage digital tools for sustainable development.

Empowering Marginalized Voices

One of the most profound impacts of digital empowerment lies in amplifying the voices of those traditionally marginalized or silenced. Digital platforms provide not only a stage but a microphone for underrepresented communities, allowing their stories to reach audiences worldwide.

Dr. Rees narrates the experiences of indigenous communities in Canada who use digital storytelling to preserve and share their cultural heritage. Employing internet archives and multimedia platforms, these communities engage in a vibrant cultural dialogue, safeguarding their languages, traditions, and histories for future generations. Through these efforts, sidelined narratives garner visibility, fostering understanding and respect across cultural divides. As digital empowerment provides a channel for expression, it simultaneously advocates for cultural preservation and recognition.

The Corporate Frontier: Responsible Tech Development

Businesses have immense potential to foster digital empowerment, serving as pivotal players in the tech landscape. By integrating ethical considerations into their operations, companies can champion accessibility, inclusivity, and user empowerment.

A leading example comes from Brazil, where a tech company partnered with local NGOs to develop applications catering to the visually impaired. Beyond just fulfilling a corporate social responsibility mandate, this initiative opened job opportunities previously unavailable to individuals with disabilities, demonstrating the transformative power of inclusive design. By championing such ethical practices, companies not only thrive economically but also contribute significantly to societal advancement.

Digital Empowerment in Crisis Situations

In times of crisis, be it natural disasters, pandemics, or socio-political upheaval, technology's catalytic role in empowerment becomes particularly pronounced. Digital tools enable communities to organize, disseminate information, and mobilize resources rapidly, often proving lifesaving.

The global COVID-19 pandemic underscored the importance of digital platforms in maintaining social connections, educational continuity, and economic stability. For instance, telemedicine became a crucial component in healthcare delivery, bridging the gap between patients and medical services in lockdown scenarios. Notably, initiatives like Project ECHO in the United States used virtual platforms to connect rural healthcare providers with specialists, enhancing healthcare delivery in underserved areas. These examples showcase the adaptability and resilience fostered by digital empowerment amidst crises.

A Practical Vision for Digital Empowerment

As we transition to the next chapter, Dr. Rees encourages readers to internalize the lessons of these narratives and examples, highlighting the tangible impacts of strategic digital empowerment. For individuals and policymakers alike, the call to action is clear: to advocate for and implement proactive measures that ensure technology remains inclusive, equitable, and empowering.

Consider the "Libraries Without Borders" initiative, a program that brings digital literacy and access to remote communities worldwide using portable digital toolkits. This project exemplifies how practical solutions can drive digital empowerment on the ground, yielding vast benefits. By providing training and infrastructure, it empowers local facilitators to disseminate knowledge and foster community development. Such initiatives illuminate the path forward, illustrating the practicality and scalability of empowerment efforts globally.

In the ensuing chapters, we will delve deeper into the legal and ethical frameworks surrounding technology's role in society. As our understanding deepens, so too will our capacity to wield digital empowerment as a tool for equitable progress, recognizing its potential to redefine human freedom on a global scale.

As we conclude Chapter 3 of Connected Rights: Reimagining

Human Freedom in the Digital Age, it is essential to reflect on the dualistic nature of technology as unveiled by Dr. Eleanor Rees. Through this exploration, we have seen that digital tools have the power both to amplify and to constrain human agency. This delicate balance challenges us to wield technology mindfully, ensuring that it serves as a beacon of empowerment rather than a mechanism of control.

We delved into the profound implications of digital communities on societal structures, observing how they break down traditional barriers and foster new avenues for participation and inclusivity. The examination of algorithms revealed their complex role in shaping decision-making processes, urging us to remain vigilant stewards of our personal narratives amidst an increasingly automated world.

Equally critical was the discourse on bridging the technological divide, highlighting the moral imperative to achieve equitable access to digital resources. The compelling case studies underscored the transformative potential of technology-driven empowerment, painting a vivid picture of individuals and communities harnessing innovation to drive social change and assert their rights.

As we transition to the next chapter, we stand at the intersection of technological possibility and ethical responsibility. Our journey ahead will navigate the legal and ethical frameworks necessary to safeguard digital rights and promote global connectivity as a universal lifeline. This forward-looking exploration invites you, the reader, to not only grasp the complexities of the digital age but to actively participate in shaping a future where technology catalyzes genuine freedom and equity for all. Let us continue with a commitment to integrating these insights into our lives and communities, moving confidently toward the societal transformation envisioned in this work.

CHAPTER 4: LEGAL FRAMEWORKS IN A DIGITAL WORLD

I n the kaleidoscopic world of rapidly evolving technologies, the question we face today is not whether our lives will be touched by digital transformations, but how deeply. As we stand on the precipice of unprecedented digital integration, we must ask: Are our legal frameworks agile enough to protect the rights and freedoms envisioned in this digital age? Chapter 4 invites you on a nuanced exploration of this vital inquiry.

The chapter unfolds with an exploration of the existing legal scaffolding that supports digital rights both domestically and internationally. It casts a spotlight on seminal laws and treaties that have paved the way for today's legal landscape, establishing the pillars upon which contemporary digital, legislative efforts stand. These foundational frameworks, while monumental in their time, now reveal how technology's relentless march forward can leave gaps waiting to be bridged.

As we journey through this chapter, we encounter the first significant challenge: the struggles of existing legal systems to adapt at the speed of technological change. Here, we delve into the limitations of traditional legal structures, uncovering a world where regulations struggle to keep pace with the digital realities that shape our daily lives. Through riveting case studies, we see the tangible impacts of this mismatch and prepare to enter discussions about the need for legal frameworks that are as dynamic and adaptable as the technology they aim to regulate.

From challenges, the chapter leads us to stories of adaptation, illustrated through poignant case studies of legal evolution to address digital rights debates. These stories are more than just academic exercises; they offer an insightful examination of real-world attempts, both successful and flawed, to weave digital rights into the fabric of existing legal systems. From privacy protection and data security to digital equity, these examples provide a window into the endeavors and complexities of crafting effective digital regulations for our present time.

The narrative then transcends national borders, emphasizing the critical need for international cooperation. In a digital sphere where connectivity knows no boundaries, the harmonization of diverse legal systems emerges as a priority. Here, we disentangle the efforts of global organizations striving to bring cohesion through mutual understanding and unified approaches, illuminating the path toward robust digital rights protection on a worldwide scale.

Finally, the chapter takes a visionary leap into the future of digital legislation. By exploring emerging technologies and their potential influence on future laws, we are guided to consider innovative, legislative approaches required to meet the demands of an ever-evolving digital landscape. This section serves as a crucial pivot, bridging ground-breaking discussions on ethics and digital equity in subsequent chapters, underscoring the continuous need for legal evolution.

Through the blend of analytical insight and Dr. Eleanor Rees's narrative prowess, Chapter 4 delivers an intricate picture of our digital world's legal frameworks. Whether you are a policy-maker, educator, or digital rights enthusiast, this chapter not only lays the foundation for understanding today's complexities but ignites a curiosity to reshape the legal future for a more inclusive, equitable digital world.

Subchapter 4.1: Overview of Current Legal Structures

In the constantly evolving digital realm, understanding the foundational legal structures that govern digital rights is crucial. These frameworks not only form the backbone of current regulatory practices but also reflect the historical journey of legislative bodies towards adapting to technological advancements. As we unfold this journey, we will trace the evolution of pivotal laws and treaties that have sculpted today's legal landscape, laying the groundwork for ongoing discussions about the future of digital legislation and rights.

1. Historical Context and Foundational Laws

From the dawn of the internet age to today's interconnected world, several key legal milestones have played a decisive role in shaping the current digital rights framework. The Computer Fraud and Abuse Act (CFAA) of 1986 in the United States marked one of the earliest attempts to address crimes related to computer technology. Although primarily focused on preventing unauthorized access to computer systems, it set a precedent for future legislation concerning digital interactions.

Simultaneously, the European Union was developing its directives on data protection. The EU Data Protection Directive, enacted in 1995, emphasized the legal rights of individuals concerning personal data processing and free movement within the EU. These early regulations laid the groundwork for what would become one of the world's strictest privacy laws: the General Data Protection Regulation (GDPR), which came into effect in 2018. While often seen as a complex regulatory framework, GDPR underscored the importance of individual privacy in the digital age, paving the way for other jurisdictions to follow suit.

In the realm of international cooperation, the formation of the International Telecommunication Union (ITU) has been crucial. Since its establishment in 1865, ITU has evolved alongside technological advancements, providing a platform for member states to collaborate on issues related to information and communication technologies (ICTs). This collaboration has been instrumental in fostering international guidelines that address ever-changing digital challenges.

2. International Treaties and Agreements

As digital technology eroded geographical boundaries, the urgent need for international cooperation became evident. The Budapest Convention on Cybercrime, adopted by the Council of Europe in 2001, marked a significant step towards creating a unified approach to combat cybercrime and protect digital rights across borders. With signatories spanning continents, the convention provided a legal framework for nations to share best practices, harmonize legislation, and collaborate on investigations of cyber offenses.

Further illustrating global collaborative efforts, the United Nations played a pivotal role in shaping internet governance through its Internet Governance Forum (IGF). Established in 2006, the IGF serves as a multi-stakeholder platform for dialogue on public policy issues related to internet governance, enhancing understanding and cooperation among countries. It has facilitated discussions on privacy, cybersecurity, and access, advocating for policies that balance individual rights with national interests.

Another noteworthy development is the World Trade Organization's (WTO) endeavors to regulate e-commerce. While the WTO's e-commerce negotiations are ongoing, the alliances formed and discussions initiated highlight the complexities of creating cohesive digital policies that respect diverse legal systems and economic stages of development.

3. National Legal Frameworks and Their Evolution

On a national level, countries have developed unique approaches to regulating digital rights, tailored to their legal traditions and societal needs. For instance, the United States has adopted a sectoral approach to privacy regulation, with specific laws addressing different industries. The Health Insurance Portability and Accountability Act (HIPAA) protects medical data, while the Children's Online Privacy Protection Act (COPPA) safeguards children's personal information.

Conversely, the European Union's approach through the GDPR offers a comprehensive framework that applies uniformly across all member states, representing a bold endeavor to harmonize privacy laws and enhance individual rights.

Emerging economies such as India and Brazil have also made significant strides in digital rights legislation. India's Information Technology Act of 2000 and Brazil's Marco Civil da Internet (Internet Bill of Rights) demonstrate the global acknowledgment of digital rights as fundamental components of modern society.

4. Case Study: GDPR – A Comprehensive Approach to Protecting Digital Rights

To illustrate the impact of foundational legal structures, let us delve into a case study on the GDPR. This regulation exemplifies how comprehensive legislation can shape digital rights paradigms globally. With its extraterritorial applicability, GDPR influenced many non-EU countries and companies, prompting them to adjust their practices to ensure compliance.

Under GDPR, concepts such as "right to be forgotten,"

data portability, and stringent consent requirements became standard. By prioritizing user control over personal data, this regulation has transformed how organizations collect, process, and store information on a scale previously unseen.

The influence of GDPR transcends borders, as seen in countries like Japan and Brazil, inspired by its principles to enhance their privacy laws. Businesses worldwide face significant penalties for non-compliance, compelling them to adopt robust data protection measures. As a result, GDPR has set a definitive benchmark for future digital rights legislation, emphasizing the balance between innovation and individual rights.

5. Practical Application: Analyzing the Impact of GDPR on Global Data Privacy Practices

A quintessential example of GDPR's global impact can be seen in its effects on international technology companies. Consider a scenario involving a fictional company, DigiTech Solutions, headquartered in the United States with operations in Europe. Prior to GDPR, DigiTech's data storage practices were solely guided by U.S. legislation. However, the enactment of GDPR prompted the organization to overhaul its data processing framework, ensuring compliance with the regulation's stringent standards.

To accomplish this, DigiTech conducted comprehensive audits of its data usage, revamped privacy policies, and implemented advanced encryption techniques. By embracing these changes, the company not only remained compliant with GDPR but also gained a competitive advantage by building trust with its international clientele through reinforced data protection assurances.

Furthermore, DigiTech's transformation illustrates the broader trend towards global harmonization of privacy laws. Many jurisdictions have adopted GDPR's principles, encouraging companies to integrate privacy-by-design into their operations, ultimately fostering a culture of digital responsibility and user empowerment worldwide.

In summary, this subchapter's exploration of the existing legal structures governing digital rights provides readers a nuanced understanding of the historical context and evolution of key laws and treaties. As we transition to the next subchapter, we delve into the challenges faced by legal systems in adapting to rapidly advancing technology, a journey that necessitates constant innovation and collaboration.

Subchapter 4.2: Challenges in Adapting Legal Systems

In an age where technology evolves at an unprecedented pace, legal systems around the world face the daunting task of adapting existing frameworks to these rapid advancements. This subchapter delves into the multifaceted challenges that arise when traditional legal structures, crafted in a pre-digital era, strive to govern the complex and dynamic world of digital rights. Dr. Eleanor Rees unpacks these challenges, illustrating the disconnect between swiftly changing digital landscapes and the slower rhythm of legislative processes.

Traditional legal systems, built upon the bedrock of tangible goods and corporeal interactions, often stumble when confronted with the intangibility of digital information and transactions. To fully grasp this challenge, consider the example of intellectual property legislation, a domain historically rooted in protecting physical creations like books, inventions, and artworks. As digital media obliterate the boundaries of replication and distribution, lawmakers find themselves grappling with questions of ownership, attribution, and enforcement in a space where content can traverse the globe with a simple click.

Sluggish Legislative Processes vs. Rapid Technological Change

One primary challenge lies in the inherently slow pace of legislative processes, which can seem glacial when juxtaposed against the speed of technological innovation. Laws often require extensive deliberation, debate, and compromises, making them inherently reactive rather than proactive. Technology, by contrast, is driven by innovation and competition, with new applications and devices emerging at breakneck speeds. By the time a legal framework is enacted, the technology it seeks to regulate may have already become obsolete or transformed.

For instance, take the case of the General Data Protection Regulation (GDPR) implemented by the European Union in 2018. While heralded as a landmark in data protection, the GDPR was years in the making. Several tech companies, anticipating such legislation, had already pivoted their business models and technologies to either comply with or circumvent these rules. Such instances manifest a persistent lag, where legislation often trails behind, responding to problems that have already fragmented into new issues by the time they are addressed.

Inflexibility of Legacy Legal Frameworks

Traditional legal frameworks are often rigid, shaped by precedents and existing doctrines that do not easily lend themselves to the fluid and cross-jurisdictional nature of digital interactions. Existing laws about privacy, security, and free expression might be tied to concepts like physical location or written communications, ill-equipped to govern an internet that is borderless and ubiquitous.

Consider the issue of data residency, where should data be 'physically' located when it exists in a cloud, a nebulous construct that spans continents? Legacy laws try to ground cyberspace interactions in physical territories, but this approach becomes problematic as more aspects of digital ecosystems, such as cloud computing and blockchain technology, decouple from any physical infrastructure.

Regulatory Gaps and Emerging Technologies

Emerging technologies often exploit regulatory gaps that exist within traditional legal systems. Cryptocurrencies, for example, emerged in the late 2000s, turning traditional financial regulations on their heads. These digital assets carve out niches that evade traditional oversight by renouncing centralized control, a hallmark of financial regulations worldwide. Similarly, social media platforms have historically resisted categorization under existing communication regulations, leading to significant challenges regarding content moderation and misinformation.

These technologies frequently bring ethical questions to the fore, such as the balance between privacy and security, or the tension between innovation and control. Without prompt and proactive adaptation, legal systems run the risk of either over-regulating nascent technologies, stifling innovation, or under-regulating, thereby failing to provide necessary protections for society.

Cultural and Jurisdictional Discrepancies

Legal systems must also contend with significant cultural and jurisdictional discrepancies. What one jurisdiction deems acceptable might be considered unacceptable elsewhere, a complexity magnified in the digital realm where actions in one part of the world can instantly impact another.

A case in point involves the varying legal stances on free speech online. In the United States, the First Amendment provides robust protections for free expression, even on digital platforms. In contrast, European countries might prioritize matters of dignity and privacy, leading to a different legal posture towards online content regulation.

Such diversity complicates the enforcement of digital laws globally. An international technology company might find itself complying with conflicting laws and regulations depending on where its services are accessed, creating a labyrinth of compliance issues.

Real-World Application: The Facebook-Cambridge Analytica Scandal

Perhaps one of the most illustrative examples of these regulatory challenges is the Facebook-Cambridge Analytica scandal. This case highlights how personal data can be harvested on a massive scale without users' explicit consent, shedding light on significant gaps within existing data protection laws at the time.

In early 2018, it was revealed that Cambridge Analytica, a political consulting firm, had collected personal information from approximately 87 million Facebook users without their consent, leveraging this data for targeted political advertising. The resultant public outcry underscored substantial inadequacies in data privacy regulations and the ability of legal frameworks to protect individuals' digital rights.

This scandal precipitated a legislative response, as regulators worldwide sought to impose stricter data privacy measures. However, it also exposed the reactive nature of legal systems, which responded only after significant consumer harm had occurred. This case exemplifies the need for laws that are agile and forward-thinking, anticipating potential rights violations rather than reacting ex post facto.

The Need for Dynamic Legal Innovation

Faced with these challenges, it becomes increasingly clear that dynamic legal innovation is essential. Legal systems must evolve towards adaptability and foresight, embracing principles of flexibility and anticipatory governance to remain effective.

The expansion of collaborative frameworks, interdisciplinary policymaking, and technological literacy among lawmakers are just steps towards this goal.

As digital landscapes continue to shift, the push for legal systems to diversify their approaches will grow stronger. By fostering rapid adaptation, legal innovation can offer robust protections for digital citizens while encouraging technological growth and development.

Transitioning from this exploration of legal challenges, the upcoming subchapter delves deeper into instances where legal structures have strived to accommodate change, featuring tangible case studies that illustrate both successes and failures in this ongoing journey towards digital legal adaptation.

Subchapter 4.3: Case Studies of Legal Adaptation

In an era where technological advances outpace legislative capabilities, the need for legal adaptation has never been more critical. As Dr. Eleanor Rees explores in this chapter, the intricate relationship between law and technology is replete with challenges and opportunities for growth. This subchapter delves into specific instances where legal frameworks have evolved to address digital rights challenges, emphasizing the lessons learned and the path forward.

To comprehend the complexities of legal adaptation in the digital realm, we must journey through a series of illuminating case studies. Each case unveils a unique facet of the adaptive process, offering valuable insights into how societies across the globe have grappled with digital rights issues such as privacy, data security, and digital equity.

General Data Protection Regulation (GDPR): A Landmark in Privacy Protection

The implementation of the General Data Protection Regulation (GDPR) by the European Union in 2018 marks one of the most significant legal adaptations in the context of digital rights. Recognizing the lag between existing privacy laws and the demands of the digital age, the GDPR was enacted to give individuals greater control over their personal data. The GDPR's stipulations extend beyond mere compliance, necessitating a transformative approach to data handling.

To comprehend the GDPR's impact, consider the case of a multinational social media company, here referred to as TechConnect, Inc. Before the GDPR, TechConnect operated multiple data centers around the world, collecting user data without prominently disclosing usage terms. With GDPR's enforcement, TechConnect had to overhaul its data management systems, implementing transparent data policies and new consent mechanisms. This required a substantial investment in legal and technical resources, illustrating the broad reach and profound impact of GDPR. As a result, TechConnect became more accountable, fostering trust with its European user base.

Yet, GDPR's resonance is not confined to the European Union. Its extraterritorial scope has prompted companies worldwide to align their practices with European standards. The ripple effect of GDPR illustrates a significant instance of legal adaptation, highlighting the regulation's influence not only in protecting privacy but also in setting a global standard.

California Consumer Privacy Act (CCPA): State-Level Innovation

On the other side of the Atlantic, the California Consumer Privacy Act (CCPA), enacted in 2020, serves as a prime example of state-level legal innovation. Although modeled after GDPR, CCPA introduced distinct elements, underscoring the potential for regional adaptations in legal frameworks.

The case of DataTrade, a Californian digital marketing firm, exemplifies the local impact of CCPA. Prior to CCPA, DataTrade collected extensive user data to tailor advertising campaigns. However, the enactment of CCPA required DataTrade to redefine its engagement strategies. The company devised a comprehensive mechanism for data request handling, enabling California residents to access, delete, or opt out of data collection. This change significantly altered DataTrade's operational model, aligning it with consumer-centric practices.

The CCPA, while primarily applicable within California, signals a shift in consumer expectations across the United States. Other states have considered similar legislations, indicating that successful adaptation does not always require uniformity but rather flexible frameworks suited to specific contexts. This adaptability underscores a broader lesson in legal evolution: legal systems must remain pliable, reflecting both regional realities and global trends.

Digital Equity in South Korea: Bridging the Divide

As one of the most technologically advanced countries, South Korea offers an instructive case study in legal adaptation, particularly in the realm of digital equity. The government, recognizing the systemic digital divide, embarked on a mission to ensure universal internet access by strengthening its legal commitments to digital infrastructure.

The case of the "Information Network Act" illustrates South Korea's proactive stance. This act incentivized the expansion of high-speed internet across the nation, with particular emphasis on reaching underserved rural communities. The initiative required collaboration with private telecom companies, backed by governmental subsidies and legal mandates. Regulations within the act ensured price controls, promoting equitable access across diverse socioeconomic segments.

One rural village in Jeollanam-do province provides a practical example of the act's success. Known for its agricultural roots and historically lacking digital access, this village saw remarkable transformation. Internet access enabled local farmers to partake in e-commerce, accessing broader markets and enhancing productivity through digital tools. The increased connectivity also facilitated educational opportunities for young residents, bridging the digital divide.

South Korea's approach highlights the potential for legal frameworks to address digital equity, ensuring technology serves as an inclusive force rather than a divisive barrier. These efforts exemplify how tailored policy interventions can incite substantial societal shifts, showcasing legal adaptation's role in fostering digital inclusion.

Intellectual Property in the Digital Age: The Napster Precedent

The advent and rise of digital file sharing during the late 1990s and early 2000s posed unprecedented challenges to intellectual property law. This conundrum is epitomized by the case of Napster, the pioneering peer-to-peer (P2P) file-sharing service. Napster enabled users worldwide to share music files freely, disrupting traditional music distribution models and prompting industry's legal response.

The legal battle culminated in the landmark case A&M Records, Inc. v. Napster, Inc., decided by the United States Court of Appeals for the Ninth Circuit in 2001. The court ruled against Napster, acknowledging its service as a contributor to copyright infringement. This judgment underscored the complexities imposed by digital technologies on intellectual property laws, propelling the legal landscape toward digital adaptation.

Post-Napster, the music industry learned to adapt by embracing digital distribution models. Services like iTunes emerged, offering legal alternatives to file-sharing. Meanwhile, subscription-based streaming, popularized by platforms like Spotify, revolutionized music consumption, aligning it with contemporary digital realities.

Napster's case remains pivotal in exploring the intersection of technology and intellectual property law, serving as a precursor to ongoing challenges in digital rights. This example underscores the necessity for legal frameworks to evolve in response to technological disruptions, illustrating how adaptive strategies can stimulate industry transformation.

Shaping Data Security Legislation: The Case of India's Personal Data Protection Bill

India's journey toward comprehensive data protection legislation offers valuable insights into the intricacies of legal adaptation. In 2019, India introduced the Personal Data Protection Bill (PDPB), reflecting an urgent need to address the complexities introduced by extensive digital engagement.

One illustrative case involves Aadhar, India's nationwide biometric identity system. Controversies surrounding data privacy led to public discourse and legal scrutiny. This prompted legislative action, aiming to safeguard personal data while balancing national interests. The PDPB, drawing inspiration from GDPR and tailored to India's context, sought to cement robust data security measures.

However, the bill's progression has faced multifaceted challenges, stemming from diverse stakeholder interests and regulatory capacities. The interplay between technological advancement and legislative response in this instance highlights the dynamism required in legal adaptation.

India's venture into expansive data protection legislation epitomizes a global quest for frameworks that both protect personal information and stimulate digital growth. It underscores the interplay between local nuances and international influences, reinforcing the interconnected nature of digital rights protection.

Legal adaptation in the digital era necessitates a nuanced understanding of diverse contexts, as illustrated by each of these case studies. Whether through privacy protections, digital equity initiatives, or intellectual property revisions, these examples reveal a common trajectory toward innovation and inclusivity. As the digital landscape continues its rapid evolution, the lessons from these cases serve as signposts, guiding future legislative endeavors.

In our next exploration, we venture into the realm of international cooperation and legal harmonization. Understanding the necessity for cohesive global frameworks, we will examine the collaborative efforts and challenges in achieving consistency in digital rights legislation across borders. An illustrative case study will illuminate the crossroads where diverse legal systems converge, offering a practical understanding of the power of unified legal action in addressing digital conundrums.

Subchapter 4.4: International Cooperation and Legal Harmonization

In today's increasingly connected world, the digital realm does not adhere to the physical borders that define nation-states. With the internet's reach transcending continents, countries find themselves interwoven in a complex web of digital interactions that require cohesive legal strategies. Subchapter 4.4 delves into the critical role of international cooperation in formulating unified legal frameworks to protect digital rights across the globe. As digital entities traverse national boundaries with ease, the pressing need for international collaboration becomes evident, prompting discussions on how disparate legal systems can synchronize to foster a comprehensive and harmonized approach to digital governance.

The Necessity for Global Collaboration

At the heart of the digital era lies a fundamental shift in how humans interact, transact, and communicate. This paradigm shift has necessitated re-evaluation of existing laws to address cross-border data flows, cybersecurity threats, and the protection of digital rights. Without global coordination, efforts to safeguard digital rights risk being fragmented and inconsistent, leading to legal loopholes and conflicting regulations. As Dr. Eleanor Rees eloquently states, "the digital age demands a degree of interconnectedness in legal structures that mirrors the boundless connectivity of the technologies we seek to regulate."

The European Union (EU) offers a pertinent example of how regional cooperation can lead to robust legal frameworks with global implications. The implementation of the General Data Protection Regulation (GDPR) in 2018 marked a significant milestone in the journey toward legal harmonization. By setting a precedent for data protection, the GDPR has influenced legislation far beyond the EU's borders, compelling companies worldwide to adhere to its stringent guidelines to engage with EU citizens. Although the GDPR represents a regional effort, its impact underscores the potential of international collaboration in crafting comprehensive legal standards.

Organizations Promoting Legal Harmonization

Several international organizations have taken the helm in steering discussions surrounding digital rights and the alignment of legal frameworks. The United Nations, through its various agencies and forums, has played a pivotal role in advocating for a human-centric approach to technology governance. The UN's International Telecommunication Union (ITU) has facilitated dialogues on global connectivity and internet governance, emphasizing the shared responsibility of member states in promoting digital rights.

Meanwhile, the World Trade Organization (WTO) has engaged in discussions about e-commerce regulations, underscoring the importance of harmonizing trade rules to facilitate seamless digital transactions. By fostering a collective understanding of digital trade policies, the WTO aims to create a conducive environment in which global digital commerce can thrive.

Addressing Challenges in Harmonization

Despite the noble intentions of these organizations, achieving complete legal harmonization remains fraught with challenges. Varied cultural, legal, and economic contexts lead to differing priorities and perceptions of digital rights. For instance, the notion of privacy holds different meanings across societies; European countries may prioritize individual privacy more stringently than others, creating tension in harmonizing privacy laws.

Moreover, countries face varying levels of technological advancement and internet penetration, influencing their capacity to implement and enforce international agreements. Bridging these technological gaps requires a concerted effort to ensure that no nation is left behind, promoting equitable participation in digital governance. As Dr. Rees notes, "the path to legal harmonization in the digital realm necessitates not only aligning legal frameworks but also fostering a shared vision of an inclusive digital future."

Steps Towards Legal Harmonization

Several steps can be taken to move toward a more harmonized global digital governance framework. First, fostering inclusive dialogues that involve all stakeholders, from governments to tech companies and civil society, ensures that diverse perspectives are considered. By engaging in multilateral discussions, countries can negotiate agreements that reflect a broad consensus and facilitate smoother implementation.

Second, building capacity in developing countries to align their digital policies with international standards is crucial. Capacity-building initiatives should focus on infrastructure development, knowledge transfer, and skill development to enable these nations to actively participate in shaping global digital policies.

Third, fostering transparency and trust among nations is essential. Trust-building measures, such as mutual recognition of digital certificates and secure data-sharing mechanisms, can pave the way for collaborative frameworks. By establishing clear and transparent processes for dispute resolution and compliance monitoring, countries can navigate the complexities of digital interactions more effectively.

Fourth, ongoing adaptation and review of international frameworks are vital in the face of evolving technologies. By embedding periodic review mechanisms within international agreements, stakeholders can ensure that legal frameworks remain relevant and responsive to technological innovations.

Practical Application: Bridging the Legal Divide in Digital Commerce

A real-world illustration of international cooperation's importance in digital law comes from the realm of digital commerce. In recent years, the global surge in e-commerce has led to increased scrutiny of cross-border online transactions. However, without standardized regulatory measures, businesses face difficulties navigating varying e-commerce laws across different jurisdictions.

The Asian region's Association of Southeast Asian Nations (ASEAN) has demonstrated how regional cooperation can alleviate these challenges. Through the ASEAN E-Commerce

Agreement, member states have outlined common principles for consumer protection, data security, and dispute resolution in online transactions. This harmonized approach not only facilitates smoother trade among ASEAN members but also positions the region as a cohesive market for international e-commerce players.

Conclusion and Transition to Subchapter 4.5

As the digital age unfolds, the call for international cooperation in legal governance becomes ever more pressing. Recognizing that digital connectivity transcends borders, this chapter underscores the significance of harmonizing diverse legal systems to ensure the consistent protection of digital rights worldwide. By fostering mutual understanding and unified approaches, countries can create a cohesive global digital landscape that prioritizes equitable participation, privacy, and security.

This exploration of international cooperation and legal harmonization sets the stage for the forthcoming subchapter on "The Future of Digital Legislation." As we peer into the future of digital rights, the narrative shifts toward strategic insights on potential evolutions in legal frameworks. Dr. Rees will examine emerging technologies poised to shape future laws, advocating for innovative legislative approaches to ensure a dynamic and equitable digital world.

Subchapter 4.5: The Future of Digital Legislation

In this forward-looking section, the narrative pivots to the future trajectories of digital legislation. Dr. Rees provides strategic insights into potential evolutions in legal frameworks designed to enhance digital rights protection. She explores emerging technologies that could shape future laws and advocates for innovative legislative approaches to meet the demands of an ever-evolving digital landscape. This subchapter serves as a bridge to the subsequent discussions on ethical considerations and digital equity in the following chapters, emphasizing the continuous need for legal adaptation.

1. The Driving Forces of Future Legislation

As technology continues to evolve at a breakneck pace, so too must the laws that govern its use and the rights of individuals within digital spaces. The proliferation of artificial intelligence, blockchain technologies, and the Internet of Things (IoT) demands that legislators not only understand these emerging technologies but also anticipate the implications they may have on society, privacy, and security.

Artificial Intelligence and Legislation

Artificial intelligence stands at the forefront of transformative technologies. Its applications, from decision-making algorithms to machine learning systems capable of autonomous operations, present both incredible opportunities and significant challenges. Legislative bodies are grappling with questions of accountability, transparency, and moral responsibility.

For example, consider the use of AI in autonomous vehicles. These cars promise decreased traffic accidents and improved mobility for individuals with disabilities. However, legislative frameworks must address the question of liability in the event of a crash. Who is responsible, the manufacturer, the programmer, or the system itself? Countries around the world are exploring various approaches. In the European Union, for instance, legislation is inclining towards strict liability on manufacturers to ensure consumer protection without stifling innovation.

Blockchain Technology

Blockchain technology presents another significant challenge. Known for its decentralized nature and use in cryptocurrencies, blockchain's potential applications extend far beyond financial transactions. Its capacity to create immutable records can revolutionize industries, from supply chain management to digital voting systems.

Countries vary in their approach to blockchain legislation. While some nations, such as Estonia, have embraced blockchain to enhance governmental transparency, others remain wary of its implications for financial regulation and security. Estonia's use of blockchain in public services demonstrates its potential, offering a case study in successful adaptation whereby citizens enjoy unfettered access to digital services with confidence in secure, tamper-proof systems.

The Internet of Things (IoT)

The IoT represents an interconnected world where devices communicate seamlessly. From smart homes to connected healthcare systems, the IoT promises convenience but also raises significant privacy and security concerns. With each device collecting potentially sensitive data, legislative frameworks must evolve to protect individual rights against breaches and misuse.

Consider a scenario where smart home devices are hacked en masse. The implications for personal security are profound, and legislators must ensure that manufacturers comply with rigorous security standards. Countries like the United States have initiated steps to create guidelines, yet a comprehensive global approach remains elusive.

2. Bridging the Gap Between Legislation and Innovation

The disparity between the rapid advancement of technology and the slower pace of legislative change requires dynamic and creative approaches to legal frameworks. Lawmakers must engage with technologists, ethicists, and society at large to create adaptive laws capable of addressing both current and emerging issues.

Collaboration with Technologists

Strategic collaboration between legislators and technologists offers a pathway to craft informed and effective legal measures. By fostering open channels of communication, lawmakers can gain insights into the implications of new technologies and anticipate challenges before they become crises.

The UK Parliament's Science and Technology Committee provides a valuable example. This body consults with experts from various technological fields to assess emerging trends and their potential legal impacts. By maintaining an ongoing dialogue, the UK is better positioned to enact laws that protect citizens while fostering innovation.

Public Engagement and Education

Successful legislative adaptation requires public involvement and education. Legislation that addresses digital rights and technology must reflect societal values and priorities, necessitating broader engagement with the public.

Consider the global response to data privacy regulations, such as the General Data Protection Regulation (GDPR) in Europe, which emerged through extensive public consultation and debate. This collaborative approach not only informed the regulation's content but also fostered greater public understanding and compliance.

3. Global Legal Harmonization: A Path Forward

The universal nature of digital technologies means that isolated legal frameworks become less effective over time. Therefore, international cooperation and legal harmonization are crucial. Global entities like the United Nations and the World Economic Forum are instrumental in facilitating these discussions but face substantial hurdles due to differing national priorities and legal traditions.

Framework Proposals for Harmonization

Proposals for a globally harmonized digital legal framework suggest a layered approach. This model envisions a set of fundamental global standards augmented by national laws tailored to individual country needs.

Such a proposal is not without precedent. International trade agreements, which balance global standards with local adaptations, offer a model. The World Trade Organization's protocols provide a framework that ensures fair trade while respecting national sovereignty, a potential analogy for digital legislation.

Challenges and Opportunities

Implementing a global legal framework presents significant challenges. Sovereign nations must reconcile their legislative autonomy with the necessity of coherence in digital rights protection. Variations in cultural values and political priorities further complicate efforts.

However, opportunities abound. By establishing universal standards, countries can foster environments conducive to innovation and investment while upholding fundamental rights. The potential for shared norms and practices offers a more predictable legal environment for global businesses and individual users alike.

Practical Application: A Case Study of Global Data Privacy Regulations

Consider the evolution of data privacy regulations as a microcosm of both the challenges and opportunities in crafting future digital legislation. The GDPR set a global benchmark by reinvigorating conversations worldwide about personal data protection.

Countries outside the European Union, such as Brazil with

its Lei Geral de Proteção de Dados (LGPD), have enacted laws mirroring GDPR principles, illustrating a trend toward legal harmonization. In the United States, debates around the Federal Trade Commission's role in data privacy mark ongoing efforts to develop a comprehensive national standard.

These initiatives highlight a critical lesson for future digital legislation: the balance between international standards and national specificity is crucial. As technologies continue to evolve, the legal frameworks governing them must remain flexible and forward-thinking, safeguarding rights while fostering innovation.

As we delve into the next chapter's exploration of the ethical implications and digital equity, this subchapter highlights how legislative agility, coupled with global collaboration, is essential in navigating the complexities of technology and law. In our interconnected world, the dialogue between innovation and regulation must remain active and adaptive, ensuring digital rights are not only protected but empowered.

As we conclude Chapter 4 on Legal Frameworks in a Digital World, we reflect on the complexities and dynamic nature of digital rights in the global landscape. This chapter has guided you through the evolution of legal structures, highlighting the landmark laws and treaties that have shaped our current understanding. You have seen the persistent challenge of aligning traditional legal systems with the relentless pace of technological advancement, as described with critical insights by Dr. Rees.

The journey through case studies offered a nuanced view of how different jurisdictions have endeavored, with varying degrees of success, to address digital rights issues like privacy and data security. This exploration underscored the importance of flexibility and innovation in shaping effective laws designed for our digital age.

International cooperation remains vital, as digital connectivity knows no borders. This chapter illuminated the necessity of unified efforts toward legal harmonization to safeguard our shared digital future. Looking ahead, the future of digital legislation promises exciting developments influenced by emerging technologies and creative policy strategies.

As you digest these insights, consider how these legal frameworks impact not only global policies but also your own digital interactions and responsibilities. Reflect on your role in this evolving narrative, whether as a citizen, policymaker, or digital user, to advocate and act towards a more equitable digital space.

Prepare to delve into the next chapter, where we will explore the ethical dimensions and digital equity that form the backbone of universal connectivity, topics that will enrich your understanding and engagement in this critical discourse. Let this be a call to action, learning, adapting, and championing connectivity as a fundamental human right in our ever-connected world.

CHAPTER 5: ETHICAL CONSIDERATIONS IN DIGITAL ACCESS

T he dawn of the digital era has sparked a revolution in how we connect, learn, and participate in the global community. Yet, as the digital world expands, it brings forth profound ethical challenges that demand our scrutiny and action. In this chapter, we embark on a critical exploration of these challenges, illuminating the ethical considerations that underpin digital access.

At the heart of our discussion is the moral imperative of digital inclusion; a clarion call echoed in the struggles for human rights throughout history. The internet today holds the key to unprecedented educational, communicative, and economic opportunities. Dr. Eleanor Rees begins by setting this ethical groundwork, challenging us to see digital inclusion not merely as an aspiration but as a duty, a necessary fight for empowerment and equality in an increasingly interconnected world.

As we navigate deeper, we encounter the shadowy complexities of surveillance and privacy in the digital age. This aspect of digital ethics probes the reshaped boundaries of personal space, as modern technology blurs the lines between security and intrusion. Herein lies an ethical dilemma: how do we harmonize the pursuit of safety and convenience with the preservation of fundamental personal freedoms? Dr. Rees deftly guides us through key incidents and policies that underscore this tension, urging a reevaluation of our digital rights.

The discourse then shifts to the realm of data rights and ownership, an area as complex as it is crucial. In an age where personal information becomes a commodity, questions of consent, control, and transparency come to the forefront. Dr. Rees meticulously dissects these issues, advocating for frameworks that protect individuals from exploitation and ensure accountability among the digital titans that dominate this new landscape.

Innovation, a powerful driver of progress and a persistent source of ethical quandaries, takes center stage next. In this exploration, Dr. Rees examines the societal impact of technological advancements, from artificial intelligence to algorithmic decision-making. The challenge lies in aligning innovation with our collective well-being, a task that requires proactive ethical guidelines and open dialogue among diverse stakeholders.

Finally, this chapter leads us to a blueprint for building ethical frameworks suited to digital societies. Dr. Rees emphasizes the collective responsibility of governments, corporations, and civil society to craft ethical standards transcending cultural and geographical boundaries. By showcasing successful international initiatives, she inspires us to engage actively in advocacy for ethically minded digital policies, setting the stage for future discussions on achieving digital equity.

Through compelling narratives and rigorous analysis, Dr. Rees calls on us to consider our roles in shaping a digital realm that honors human dignity. This chapter invites readers to ponder how they can contribute to a future where ethical considerations in digital access are not just a topic of discussion but a cornerstone of our global community. It is a call to action, challenging us to champion a digital society in which connectivity empowers and uplifts all.

Subchapter 5.1: The Moral Imperative of Digital Inclusion

In the kaleidoscope of human progress, the digital revolution represents a pivotal shift comparable to historical epochs such as the Renaissance or the Industrial Revolution. Yet, unlike these, the digital age holds profound implications for human rights, reaching into every sphere of life with incredible potential and formidable challenges. Among these lies a compelling ethical obligation that has increasingly gained attention: digital inclusion. Dr. Eleanor Rees, with her background in digital anthropology, draws upon historical movements for human rights to argue that the internet, with its unparalleled provision for education, communication, and economic opportunity, is not merely a luxury but a moral imperative that every individual deserves.

Digital Access as a Human Right

To begin this exploration, we must first dissect the fundamental question: why should digital access be viewed as a human right? Historically, human rights movements have focused on removing barriers, whether societal, economic, or political, to ensure equitable access to opportunities. The Civil Rights Movement in the United States during the 1960s serves as a poignant illustration, highlighting how access to education, voting, and public spaces were fundamentally linked to broader notions of justice and equity. In parallel, the digital age demands a similar reevaluation of what constitutes access aside from these traditional domains.

In today's world, access to the internet is as vital as access to education in the past. It acts as a bridge connecting individuals to the vast repository of global knowledge. Educational platforms like Khan Academy and Coursera democratize learning, offering courses across a plethora of disciplines to anyone with internet access. Imagine a young girl in a remote village in India who, via the internet, can gain an education previously inaccessible to her due to geography or economic constraints. This transformative power makes digital access not just an opportunity but a moral duty to ensure worldwide.

Philosophical Foundations: Equality and Justice

The philosophical underpinnings of this obligation are deeply rooted in the principles of equality and justice. The philosophical doctrines of John Rawls and Amartya Sen provide a compelling basis for understanding why digital inclusion should transcend mere policy and enter the realm of ethical imperatives.

Rawls' theory of justice advocates for a society where inequalities must be arranged to benefit the least advantaged; his "difference principle" intrinsically supports the notion of digital equity. By ensuring that everyone has equal access to digital tools, we minimize disparities in information and resource distribution, fostering a society more aligned with Rawlsian justice. Similarly, Sen's capabilities approach underscores the importance of enhancing individual capabilities through equitable access to resources, precisely what digital inclusion accomplishes on a global scale.

The ethical groundwork laid by these philosophical perspectives paves the way for comprehensive policies and practices that prioritize digital inclusion. As Dr. Rees asserts, when we anchor digital access within the framework of equality and justice, we not only empower disenfranchised communities but also promote a more equitable society.

The Transformative Impact of Digital Inclusion

To elaborate on why digital inclusion constitutes an ethical necessity, it is essential to highlight its transformative impact across various sectors. In economic terms, access to digital platforms can be a powerful equalizer. For instance, micro-entrepreneurs in rural Kenya are leveraging mobile banking systems like M-Pesa to conduct business without the need for traditional banking infrastructure. Such platforms facilitate commerce, enable savings, and provide financial security, transforming lives by implementing a more inclusive economy.

In the healthcare sector, telemedicine stands as a testament to digital access' life-saving potential. Consider a rural area with limited medical facilities, through digital platforms, patients can consult specialists across the globe, acquiring necessary diagnoses and treatments that were once out of reach. The introduction of telemedicine initiatives in countries like Brazil has significantly improved health outcomes and reduced inequities in healthcare access.

Inside the political arena, digital access can redefine civic participation. Social media platforms and online forums provide individuals with the tools to engage in public discourse and advocate for change. Grassroots movements, powered through digital connectivity, such as the Arab Spring or Hong Kong's pro-democracy protests, underscore the internet's role as a catalyst for political engagement and reform. This newfound ability to amplify voices from the margins onto a global stage fortifies the argument that digital inclusion is a mechanism for societal transformation.

Real-World Example: The E-Estonia Model

To encapsulate the real-world applicability of these ideas, the case of Estonia, a digital pioneer, illustrates the potential of comprehensive digital inclusion. Labelled as e-Estonia, this

Northern European nation has redefined citizenship through digitalization. Nearly all government services are accessible online, ranging from voting to medical prescriptions to tax filings. Estonia's e-Residency program even extends its digital benefits globally, allowing non-residents to establish and operate businesses within a secure online ecosystem.

Such integration not only boosts national efficiency and transparency but significantly contributes to social inclusivity. With free public Wi-Fi hotspots widespread across the country and a strong emphasis on digital education, Estonia ensures that its citizens, regardless of age or socioeconomic status, are equipped to thrive in an increasingly digital world. This approach demonstrates the substantial benefits that can ensue when a nation commits to digital inclusion as an ethical priority.

Practical Application: Bridging the Gap in Local Communities

Taking inspiration from successful national models, smaller communities and local governments can embark on journeys towards digital inclusion by focusing on three key strategies: infrastructure development, policy reform, and digital literacy education.

1. Infrastructure Development: Initiatives should prioritize expanding affordable internet services, particularly in underserved rural areas. Public-private partnerships can be instrumental in achieving this goal by combining technological expertise with robust funding sources.

2. Policy Reform: To foster an inclusive digital environment, it is vital to craft policies that promote equitable access and protect against digital monopolies. Local governments should enact regulations that incentivize competition and innovation within the telecommunications sector, ensuring fair pricing and service delivery.

3. Digital Literacy Education: Programs aimed at enhancing

digital literacy can empower communities to utilize technology effectively, fostering skills that are essential for personal and professional development. For instance, the establishment of community tech hubs, akin to public libraries, could provide training sessions, workshops, and resources that enable individuals to navigate digital tools confidently.

As the conversation transitions into the subsequent subchapter on surveillance and privacy, these practical applications of digital inclusion underscore the ethical imperative to dismantle barriers in the digital realm, a mission that intricately connects with ensuring personal freedoms in a surveilled society. This layered understanding of digital inclusion sets the stage for deeper reflections on how we navigate privacy and individual rights in the face of increasing digital interconnectivity.

Subchapter 5.2: Surveillance and Privacy in the Digital Age

In the interconnected world of the digital age, the concepts of surveillance and privacy have taken on complex new dimensions, reshaping the way individuals perceive personal space and freedom. Dr. Eleanor Rees, with her deep-rooted expertise in digital anthropology, brings a nuanced perspective to these evolving ethical challenges. At the heart of this subchapter lies an exploration of the ethical implications stemming from modern surveillance technologies and widespread data collection practices. These issues, often justified under the pretexts of security and user convenience, have sparked profound debates concerning the balance between individual privacy rights and the expansive power wielded by states and corporations.

In recent years, the digital environment has made it increasingly difficult to maintain traditional boundaries surrounding privacy. The pervasive presence of surveillance technologies, from CCTV cameras in public spaces to sophisticated algorithms tracking online behavior, challenges long-held notions of anonymity and autonomy. Consider the brief example of CCTV surveillance in London, a city known for having one of the highest concentrations of surveillance cameras worldwide. While these cameras are intended to deter and investigate crime, they simultaneously lead to a reduction in individuals' expectations of privacy in public arenas.

Such surveillance activities raise critical ethical dilemmas. On one hand, the promise of safety through surveillance is appealing, as it purports to offer enhanced security. On the other, the potential for abuse and erosion of civil liberties is significant, as increased surveillance often leads to unchecked government power. Dr. Rees implores us to weigh these conflicting priorities and emphasizes that this balance must not come at the expense of individual rights.

Statistics and factual situations bring these issues into sharper focus. For instance, the United States' Patriot Act, enacted after the September 11 attacks, expanded surveillance powers significantly, enabling the government to conduct extensive electronic monitoring of communication such as emails, phone calls, and internet activity without traditional checks and balances. This policy, while aimed at preventing further terrorist activities, sparked sharp debate over its encroachment on civil liberties, with critics arguing the measures were excessive and constituted a violation of privacy.

Equally pertinent is the role of corporations in surveillance, often through the guise of data collection for personalized advertising. The case of Cambridge Analytica serves as a prime example, where personal data from millions of Facebook users was harvested without their explicit consent to influence political campaigns. This incident highlights the moral quandaries associated with the commodification of personal information and underscores the urgent need for greater accountability and ethical conduct within the digital space.

Globally, this issue has been met with varied responses. The European Union, for instance, implemented the General Data Protection Regulation (GDPR) as a comprehensive policy framework to uphold consumer privacy rights and impose stringent data handling standards on organizations. By mandating clear consent for data usage and providing individuals with the right to access and erase their data, the GDPR represents a pioneering approach to safeguarding privacy. Dr. Rees views this as an essential step, although she acknowledges that legislation must continue to evolve alongside technological advancements to remain effective.

As we navigate this landscape, Dr. Rees encourages a proactive, informed approach to privacy in the digital age. Individuals must educate themselves on the extent and implications of surveillance technologies, advocating for transparency and ethical oversight. There is also a growing need for public discourse that encompasses ethicists, legal experts, policymakers, and technologists to forge pathways toward common ground where privacy concerns and security interests align.

A relevant scenario that illustrates this dialogue is the burgeoning use of biometric identification technologies at airports for quicker, seamless boarding experiences, a convenience valued by travelers. However, these systems, which collect and compare facial, fingerprint, or iris data, raise serious concerns about consent, data security, and surveillance creep. For instance, a widely cited incident occurred when a U.S. airport reportedly began using facial recognition technology without explicitly informing passengers or providing an easy opt-out option, resulting in public backlash and a subsequent demand for greater transparency and regulation.

In the face of such ethical dilemmas, the importance of

informed policy crafting and ethical technology design cannot be overstated. By fostering conversations around what true informed consent should encompass and how to protect individual privacy rights, society can begin to address these modern challenges head-on.

As this subchapter concludes, Dr. Rees gently leads us into the next discussion, where the ethical considerations around data ownership and rights will be explored. She challenges us to consider not only who holds the keys to our personal information but also who benefits from its use. Through understanding and interrogation of these concepts, readers are empowered to participate actively in shaping the digital future.

To close, consider the example of "Sidewalk Labs," a Google subsidiary planning to develop a "smart city" based on the integration of cutting-edge technology in Toronto, Canada. The project envisaged leveraging widespread sensor deployment and data collection to optimize city operations and improve the quality of life. Yet, amidst potential innovation breakthroughs, it faces considerable criticism and opposition from privacy advocates concerned with the quantity of personal data collected and managed. This ongoing dialogue serves as a learning platform for numerous stakeholders globally, emphasizing the significant role of collaborative engagement in addressing the tension between collective advancement and individual privacy.

Subchapter 5.3: Data Rights and Ownership

In today's interconnected world, the topic of data rights and ownership is not only timely but also critical. As individuals' interactions in the digital realm continue to grow exponentially, so does the volume of data being generated, collected, and analyzed. The digital economy thrives on this data, leveraging it in ways unimaginable just a few decades ago. Yet, the crux of this evolution lies in the ethical questions surrounding who owns this data, how it is used, and what rights individuals have over their personal information.

Dr. Eleanor Rees begins her examination of data rights with a fundamental question: When we engage in digital activities, do we truly understand the extent to which we relinquish control over our personal data? She highlights that the commodification of data has made it one of the most valuable assets in the modern economy. In the face of this digital commodification, the nuances of consent, control, and ownership become increasingly complex and contested.

The conversation around data rights often centers on the principle of informed consent. However, Dr. Rees points out that what passes as consent in today's digital interactions is frequently neither fully informed nor genuinely voluntary. For instance, consider the ubiquity of lengthy terms and conditions agreements that accompany most online services. These documents are notoriously dense and often opaque, effectively discouraging users from fully understanding what they agree to. As a result, individuals may unwittingly cede control over their data. The imbalance of power between users who provide data and corporations that collect it is striking and calls for a deeper ethical inquiry.

To illustrate these intricacies, Dr. Rees examines the Facebook-Cambridge Analytica scandal, a watershed moment in public awareness of data privacy issues. The scandal unveiled how personal data collected through seemingly innocent apps could be harnessed for manipulative purposes without explicit user consent. This incident dramatically emphasized the need for stronger ethical frameworks that prioritize user rights and establish clear guidelines for data usage.

Yet, even as the scandal prompted regulatory responses,

such as the introduction of the European Union's General Data Protection Regulation (GDPR), challenges persist. These regulations, while a step in the right direction, highlight the complexities of implementing data rights protections across different jurisdictions with varying legal standards and cultural attitudes toward privacy.

Dr. Rees further explores how the concept of ownership is evolving in the digital age. Traditionally, ownership connoted having exclusive rights and control over a tangible object. In the digital realm, however, ownership becomes more nuanced. When users upload photos to social media, for instance, they frequently grant the platform a broad license to use their images, often without realizing the full extent of this agreement. This shift from tangible ownership to digital licensing agreements demands a reevaluation of what ownership means and how it should be respected.

Within this discourse, the importance of transparency and accountability in data handling practices cannot be overstated. Organizations must be clear about how they collect, store, and use data, ensuring that users can easily understand and access this information. Dr. Rees underscores the ethical necessity for companies to adopt a 'privacy by design' approach, integrating data protection principles into the core of their operations rather than as an afterthought.

To navigate these complex issues, Dr. Rees advocates for the empowerment of individuals through education and engagement. Digital literacy becomes paramount in enabling users to understand their rights and exercise more control over their personal information. This includes raising awareness about the existence and implications of data mining and profiling techniques.

Moreover, Dr. Rees highlights the need for proactive participation from civil society, academia, and individuals in shaping the discourse around data rights. These stakeholders can play a critical role in advocating for policies that protect consumers and promote ethical practices.

A compelling real-life case study that reinforces these themes is the New Zealand government's approach to data privacy. New Zealand has been recognized for its efforts to enhance data protection by creating transparent processes and engaging citizens in discussions about data use policies. Through public consultations and policy reviews, the government emphasizes accountability and fosters trust among its citizens. This model underscores how transparent governance and active civic engagement can create an environment where data rights are respected and protected.

In conclusion, while the digital economy offers immense opportunities for innovation and growth, it also necessitates a reevaluation of traditional concepts of ownership and control. As Dr. Rees adeptly notes, navigating the ethical terrain of data rights requires a collaborative and conscious effort to balance technological advancement with respect for individual rights. As we transition into the next subchapter, we will explore how these ethical considerations intertwine with the broader implications of technological innovation, examining the delicate balance between progress and societal impact.

Subchapter 5.4: Navigating Ethical Dilemmas in Technological Innovation

In today's world, technology evolves with striking speed, altering how we interact, learn, and operate within society. The innovations we witness, be it in artificial intelligence, biometric data, or algorithmic decision-making, come with undeniable benefits and equal measure of challenges. Dr. Eleanor Rees delves into the intricate dance between technological advancement and ethical integrity, exploring the gray areas where human values must coexist with digital prowess.

The journey begins with an exploration into artificial intelligence (AI), a field that represents both extraordinary potential and significant ethical complexity. From chatbots that converse with us as naturally as friends to algorithms that diagnose diseases more accurately than physicians, AI's capabilities can bolster productivity, save lives, and enrich human experiences. However, alongside these advantages lie ethical questions, particularly regarding bias ingrained in AI systems. Dr. Rees challenges readers to consider scenarios where AI, designed through datasets reflecting human prejudices, makes decisions that may inadvertently perpetuate or exacerbate societal inequalities.

For instance, consider the case of AI in hiring practices. Imagine a company utilizing an AI-driven recruitment tool to streamline its application process. If this AI system is trained on biased data, perhaps historical hiring patterns that favored one demographic over others, it may continue to mirror that bias, inadvertently discriminating against equally qualified candidates from diverse backgrounds. This perpetuation of bias exemplifies the ethical responsibility that developers, companies, and society bear in ensuring that technology evolves equitably.

Moving to biometric data, the discussion centers on technologies that have profoundly transformed security and identification processes. Tools that rely on fingerprint, facial recognition, and iris scans offer unparalleled security advantages. Yet, they also raise pressing concerns about privacy, consent, and surveillance. The implications of biometric data collection highlight a crucial ethical dilemma: the balance between technological convenience and individual autonomy.

Dr. Rees draws on a real-world example from nation-state

surveillance practices. In some countries, biometric data is collected on a massive scale under the guise of national security. While these measures aim to bolster safety and streamline governmental processes, they can also lead to pervasive state monitoring, opening the door to potential misuse or abuse of personal data without the individual's knowledge or consent.

To humanize such a complex issue, consider a hypothetical citizen, "Ayaan," living in a country where biometric checks are standard for access to public services. While Ayaan appreciates the efficiency, she grapples with concerns over how her data is used, who has access, and whether her privacy is truly safeguarded. Ayaan's dilemma illuminates the ethical tightrope walked by policymakers tasked with protecting public good without encroaching on personal freedoms.

Algorithmic decision-making, another facet of technological innovation, also faces scrutiny from an ethical standpoint. Whether determining credit scores, recommending parole, or curating news feeds, algorithms influence critical aspects of life. Dr. Rees emphasizes the need for transparency, accountability, and fairness in these decisions, lest their opaque nature perpetuate existing societal biases or create new forms of discrimination.

Consider a commonplace example of algorithmic decision-making: the algorithm-driven news feed on social media platforms. These algorithms, designed to maximize user engagement, can inadvertently create echo chambers, reinforcing users' pre-existing beliefs and skewing perceptions of reality. Dr. Rees presents a compelling argument for stakeholders to embrace ethical frameworks that demand visibility into how these algorithms function, ensuring they contribute positively to informed discourse rather than divisively fragmenting it.

The ethical quandaries inherent in these technological

advancements necessitate proactive measures and collaborative efforts. Dr. Rees advocates for a multilateral approach, calling upon technologists, ethicists, policymakers, and the public to engage in open dialogues and craft guidelines that align technological innovation with human values. This consensus-building process can bridge gaps, offering a path forward where ethical integrity and technological potential coexist symbiotically.

A vibrant case study that echoes this ethos is the European Union's General Data Protection Regulation (GDPR). Through its stringent data protection and privacy laws, GDPR exemplifies a robust framework aiming to harmonize corporate innovation with respect for individual rights. By mandating transparency in data usage and providing individuals more control over their personal data, GDPR stands as a testament to what collaborative, ethically guided policy-making can achieve.

As Dr. Rees underscores, navigating ethical dilemmas in technological innovation is not a passive endeavor but an ongoing, dynamic responsibility. The dialogue initiated in this subchapter sets the stage for further exploration into how society can collectively mold technologies that advance humanity without compromising fundamental rights. Transitioning to Subchapter 5.5, the text will explore constructing ethical frameworks that empower digital societies, ensuring inclusivity, equity, and justice within the digitally connected world.

Subchapter 5.5: Building an Ethical Framework for Digital Societies

As the digital revolution accelerates, societies worldwide grapple with the formidable challenge of aligning technological advancements with ethical principles. Building an ethical framework for digital societies is not only a necessity but a pressing demand of our times. This quest for digital morality embodies a collective journey that transcends borders, requiring collaborative effort from governments, corporations, civil society, and individuals alike. Dr. Eleanor Rees, in her characteristic eloquence and insight, guides us through this intricate process, highlighting the significance of ethical alignment in a rapidly digitizing world.

At the core of this endeavor is the question: what constitutes an ethical framework in the digital age? To answer this, we must first acknowledge the profound influence of digital technologies on every facet of human existence. From altering how we communicate and access information to reshaping economies and cultural narratives, technology has become a vital thread in our societal fabric. Therefore, crafting ethical standards involves understanding these multifaceted influences and ensuring they align with humanity's core values such as dignity, equality, and justice.

Governments play a pivotal role in this framework by crafting legislation that governs the ethical use of digital technologies. However, the dynamic nature of technological innovation challenges traditional regulatory approaches. Policymakers must become more agile and tech-savvy, understanding the nuances of emerging technologies such as artificial intelligence, blockchain, and quantum computing. A proactive approach involves creating flexible yet robust regulations that can adapt to new technological paradigms. Furthermore, international cooperation is paramount, as digital boundaries blur national borders, necessitating coordinated global efforts to uphold ethical standards universally.

Corporations, as key drivers of technological innovation, carry the responsibility of integrating ethical considerations into their business models. Ethical digital practice begins at the conceptual stage and continues through development and deployment. Companies should adopt a values-driven approach, embedding frameworks that promote transparency, accountability, and user-centricity. Ethical business practices extend beyond compliance, focusing on creating technologies that empower users rather than exploit them. Building trust with users involves clear communication about data usage, robust security measures, and a commitment to redress mechanisms when breaches occur.

Civil society, comprising non-governmental organizations, advocacy groups, and individuals, serves as the conscience of digital societies. These entities play a crucial watchdog role, holding governments and corporations accountable for ethical lapses. By raising awareness, educating the public, and advocating for digital rights, civil society invigorates the ethical dialogue, ensuring it remains grounded in the principles of human dignity and social justice. Grassroot movements often spark significant shifts, as seen in cases where public outcry has led to legislative changes, highlighting the power of collective voice in shaping digital ethics.

A crucial element of building this framework lies in cultivating ethical literacy among citizens. Informed and vigilant digital citizens are indispensable to the health of digital societies. Education systems must integrate ethical digital practices into their curricula, preparing future generations to navigate technological landscapes responsibly. Initiatives like community workshops, digital ethics campaigns, and online resources can empower individuals of all ages, fostering a society that values and practices digital ethics in both personal and professional contexts.

It is worth examining successful international collaborations as tangible evidence of the potential for building global ethical standards. The General Data Protection Regulation (GDPR) implemented by the European Union exemplifies a comprehensive approach to digital ethics, protecting individual data rights while setting a benchmark for global standards.

Its ripple effects are visible worldwide, influencing privacy laws and corporate data policies across continents. However, as Dr. Rees advises, adopting similar frameworks requires adaptability, ensuring that they respect local contexts and cultural values while maintaining core ethical principles.

The Digital Geneva Convention is another illustrative case, proposing an international framework to protect cyberspace from warfare, safeguarding critical infrastructure from digital attacks. Such collaborative efforts exemplify the spirit of shared responsibility, illustrating how diverse stakeholders can unite in pursuit of a common ethical vision. However, for these initiatives to succeed, they must be rooted in genuine commitment and continual dialogue among stakeholders, agile enough to respond to technological evolution.

Eleanor Rees emphasizes that building an ethical framework is as much about process as it is about outcomes. It requires fostering a culture of continuous reflection and adaptation, where stakeholders remain open to learning from past experiences, sharing best practices, and modifying approaches in response to new ethical challenges. Innovation must be married with foresight, anticipating not just technological possibilities but the ethical implications they entail.

To illustrate the practical application of building ethical frameworks, consider the case study of Estonia, a digital society renowned for its integrated approach to digital ethics and innovation. Estonia's e-Residency program epitomizes how ethical frameworks can foster inclusivity and economic opportunity while safeguarding digital rights. By providing a digital identity to global citizens, the program enables individuals to start businesses and engage in cross-border commerce, showcasing the potential of digital inclusion within an ethical framework. Estonia's approach integrates transparency and security, offering users rigorous privacy protections and empowering them with control over personal data. The collaborative effort among government, businesses, and citizens to maintain trust and uphold ethical standards in digital practices offers valuable lessons for other nations navigating similar digital transformations.

As we weave ethical considerations into the digital tapestry, the conclusion of this subchapter leads seamlessly into broader discussions about the future of digital equity and empowerment. Dr. Rees prepares us to explore how ethical governance, informed by collaborative frameworks, can drive societal transformation toward a more equitable digital age. Just as Estonia exemplifies the power of ethical frameworks in practice, so too can other regions and communities develop tailored approaches that reflect shared values, creating a global tapestry of ethical digital societies.

As we conclude Chapter 5, the profound ethical considerations in digital access emerge as both a challenge and an opportunity in our interconnected world. Dr. Rees has guided us through a transformative journey, beginning with the moral imperative for digital inclusion, a call to action that aligns with the historic struggle for equality and human rights. This foundational principle advocates for universal internet access as an empowering tool for marginalized communities worldwide.

We then traversed the intricate landscape of privacy and surveillance, where digital boundaries are continually tested. This exploration revealed the pressing need to protect individual freedoms against the ever-expanding reach of state power and corporate interests. Dr. Rees's insights compel us to recognize the critical balance between security and personal freedom.

Advancing to the discourse on data rights and ownership, we were introduced to the complex dynamics of consent and control in the digital realm. The necessity for robust legal protections to shield against data exploitation resonates as a clarion call for ethical foresight and transparency.

Furthermore, the ethical dilemmas posed by rapid technological innovation highlight the importance of proactive collaboration among stakeholders. Dr. Rees's examination of these issues demonstrates the need for ethical guidelines to ensure technology serves humanity's best interests.

Finally, the chapter charts a path toward building an ethical framework for digital societies, emphasizing global collaboration and advocacy for ethical digital policies. This foundation sets the stage for the upcoming chapter, where we will delve into achieving digital equity and empowerment through ethical governance. As we navigate forward, the potential to harness digital technology ethically and inclusively beckons us to redefine our roles in the digital age, fostering a more equitable and inclusive future for all.

CHAPTER 6: DIGITAL EQUITY AND ACCESS

I n an age where the digital realm holds unprecedented potential to shape futures, the promise of a connected world remains tantalizingly out of reach for many. Chapter 6: Digital Equity and Access invites us to confront one of the most pressing challenges of our time, the stark disparities in digital access that persist even as technology advances at a breathtaking pace. It is a journey into understanding how these disparities undermine the very foundation of equal opportunity and socio-economic progress. As we peel back the layers of digital inequity, we uncover not only the barriers that exclude millions but also the tangible solutions that can pave the way toward a digitally inclusive society.

At the heart of this chapter lies the concept of the digital divide. Subchapter 6.1 guides us in unpacking this complex issue, examining how it manifests across different regions and populations. Through an exploration of the economic, geographic, and educational dimensions of the divide, we gain a deeper appreciation for the systemic nature of this challenge. Statistical insights and global perspectives reveal the stark realities faced by those on the wrong side of this divide, highlighting the implications for education, economic development, and social inclusion.

Building on this foundation, Subchapter 6.2 investigates the barriers that perpetuate digital inequity. From infrastructure limitations to socio-economic challenges and the persistent rural-urban divide, we delve into the myriad factors that contribute to unequal access. Case studies and real-world examples illustrate how these barriers manifest in varied contexts, underscoring the urgency of bridging these divides to foster a truly inclusive digital landscape.

As we transition to solutions, Subchapter 6.3 provides a beacon of hope. It showcases innovative strategies and initiatives from around the world aimed at promoting digital equity. From governmental policies to the efforts of nonprofits and the private sector, these stories reflect the dynamic and multifaceted approaches being employed to enhance internet access and digital literacy. Successful case studies highlight effective methodologies and innovations, proving that scalable and sustainable solutions are not only possible but already making an impact.

Education, a cornerstone of empowerment, takes center stage in Subchapter 6.4. Here, we examine its critical role in bridging the digital gap, exploring how digital literacy initiatives and educational policies can transform underserved populations. By analyzing programs that integrate technology into curricula, we witness the potential impact on student outcomes and community development, recognizing that empowering educators is a vital step in this process.

Finally, Subchapter 6.5 paints a vision of a digitally inclusive future. Imagining a world where digital access is a universal norm, we reflect on the collaborative efforts needed from governments, corporations, and civil society to make this vision a reality. The socio-economic and cultural benefits of comprehensive digital inclusion are profound, empowering citizens and fostering equitable growth.

Chapter 6 is not merely a dialogue on disparities but a call to action, a reminder of the collective responsibility we hold in pursuing digital equity as a fundamental human right. As we advance through these subchapters, let us be inspired to participate in shaping a future where connectivity is not a privilege but a shared promise of progress for all.

Subchapter 6.1: Understanding the Digital Divide

As we embark on comprehensively exploring digital equity and access, our understanding must begin with the digital divide, a complex and persistent phenomenon that underscores substantial gaps in digital access across various demographic groups. The digital divide encapsulates a range of disparities, including economic, geographic, and educational differences, that collectively influence individuals' and communities' ability to participate in the digital age. In this subchapter, we will delve deeper into the roots and implications of this divide, examining the extent of its impact on economic development, education, and social inclusion globally. We will support our discussion with statistical analyses, practical examples, and real-life case studies to anchor our understanding in tangible realities.

To begin with, the digital divide can be succinctly defined as the gap between individuals, households, businesses, and geographic areas with various levels of access to information and communication technologies (ICT) and the internet. This divide manifests in several dimensions. Economically, it speaks to the disparity between those who can afford digital devices and internet connectivity and those who cannot. Geographically, it highlights the differences between urban areas, typically well-connected, and rural or remote regions, where such access may be severely limited. Educationally, it includes the contrast between individuals with sufficient digital literacy, a critical skill set in today's world, and those lacking the knowledge and ability to effectively use digital tools.

Economic Disparities

The economic dimension of the digital divide is perhaps the most visible. Internet connectivity is often perceived as a basic utility, akin to electricity or water, yet the economic barriers remain significant. According to a 2021 report from the International Telecommunication Union (ITU), nearly 50% of the world's population is still offline. This startling statistic illustrates a global economic disparity where considerable portions of society remain cut off from digital participation simply because they cannot afford the necessary technology or subscription fees. The report further notes that the cost of internet connectivity relative to income is substantially higher in developing nations, exacerbating the problem. For instance, in regions where income inequality is pronounced, access to the internet can be out of reach for low-income households, effectively excluding them from the digital economy and hindering opportunities for socioeconomic advancement.

Geographic Disparities

Geographic disparities are another significant factor contributing to the digital divide. The contrast between urban and rural areas in terms of internet access is stark. Urban centers tend to benefit from high-speed broadband infrastructure due to concentrated investment and greater economic incentives for service providers. Conversely, many rural and remote areas are still reliant on outdated or non-existent infrastructure. In some parts of sub-Saharan Africa, for instance, the lack of physical infrastructure remains a formidable barrier, with satellite internet being one of the few viable but costly options. This geographic digital divide means that inhabitants of rural areas miss out on numerous benefits, from telehealth services and remote education to digital commerce and e-governance.

This lack of access translates into reduced opportunities, further entrenching rural communities in cycles of poverty and marginalization.

Educational Disparities

On the educational front, digital literacy marks a crucial divide. Even where physical access to digital tools and the internet is available, a lack of skills can render these resources useless. Digital literacy encompasses a range of competencies, including the ability to use devices, software, and applications effectively, understanding of online safety and privacy, and the critical capacity to evaluate information online. Without these skills, individuals are unable to fully participate in digital environments. This educational gap is often observed in schools that lack the resources or curricula to teach digital skills adequately. In developing countries, where educational systems might already be under strain, the integration of digital literacy into education becomes even more challenging.

A compelling example is India, where a burgeoning economy showcases significant technological advancement yet grapples with a notable digital divide. While urban centers like Bangalore and Mumbai thrive as tech hubs, rural areas suffer from inadequate ICT infrastructure and educational disparities. Efforts to distribute laptops to students in rural schools have highlighted an educational challenge: students often receive devices without prior computer literacy training, limiting the initiative's effectiveness.

Implications on Economic Development, Education, and Social Inclusion

The digital divide's implications extend beyond individual inconveniences, affecting broader societal domains such as economic development, education, and social inclusion. Economically, the divide constrains potential growth by excluding large segments of the population from participating in digital economies. Without reliable internet, countless entrepreneurs and small businesses cannot reach new markets, limiting innovation and economic contributions.

Educationally, the digital divide results in unequal access to learning resources. During the COVID-19 pandemic, this inequity was starkly highlighted as schools shifted to online platforms globally. Students in well-connected areas continued their education relatively seamlessly, while those lacking connectivity were left behind, worsening educational inequalities. UNESCO reports have underscored the long-term impact of such disruptions on future employment opportunities and economic productivity for affected students.

Socially, the digital divide impairs community inclusion and participation in contemporary civic life. Access to information, social networks, and digital communication channels form the backbone of modern social interaction. When communities or individuals are excluded from these networks, their capacity to engage with societal change diminishes. For instance, digital exclusion can prevent marginalized groups from organizing effectively for social causes or accessing essential government services delivered online. The resulting social isolation can reinforce existing societal barriers, making it challenging to address complex social issues collaboratively.

Global Manifestations of the Digital Divide

To truly appreciate the global scale of the digital divide, it is essential to explore its diverse manifestations across different regions and contexts. In developed nations like the United States, the divide often appears along economic and racial lines; marginalized communities such as African-American and Hispanic populations, along with low-income households, experience lower levels of internet access. Conversely, in developing regions, the divide is more affected by infrastructure deficits and a lack of affordable services.

Case studies exemplifying these disparities include the ongoing 'Internet for All' initiative in various African nations where partnerships between governments, telecommunication companies, and international organizations aim to extend internet access to remote communities. In Uganda, the establishment of community networks has empowered local residents, reducing costs by using unlicensed spectrum frequencies, allowing a cooperative model of internet access that benefits the whole community. Similarly, initiatives such as the Alliance for Affordable Internet work towards advocating reduced data costs and the development of policies that prioritize digital inclusion.

Practical Application

An effective method to engage readers with the concept of the digital divide is by illustrating real-life scenarios that depict common challenges faced due to this gap. Consider a small, rural agricultural business in Brazil's northeastern region struggling to access crop market data due to poor internet connectivity. This limitation severely limits the farmer's ability to make informed decisions regarding production and sales, ultimately impacting profit margins. However, government-led initiatives, such as establishing digital hubs in rural areas, have begun to change this narrative. By providing reliable internet access and digital training, these hubs empower local farmers with the tools to engage more competitively in broader markets, directly addressing the digital divide and promoting economic growth.

The digital divide remains an urgent global issue, necessitating concerted efforts and innovative solutions to bridge the gaps in access and capability. As we transition to the next subchapter, we will further dissect the barriers contributing to this divide, setting the stage for a comprehensive exploration of methods and strategies designed to foster digital equity.

Subchapter 6.2: Barriers
to Digital Access

In a world increasingly defined by digital connectivity, access to technology and the internet is no longer a luxury but a fundamental necessity. Yet, despite the acknowledgment of its importance, digital access remains an elusive reality for millions worldwide. This subchapter delves into the principal barriers that perpetuate digital divides, revealing how infrastructure limitations, socio-economic factors, and the rural-urban dichotomy contribute to the persistent gaps in digital access.

The realm of digital access is fraught with complexities that mirror broader socio-economic disparities. While the internet is often heralded as a democratizing tool, providing unprecedented access to information and opportunities, the barriers to entry reveal a starkly different narrative. A fundamental challenge lies in the infrastructure required to support digital access. In many parts of the world, particularly in remote and under-resourced regions, basic infrastructure such as reliable electricity and telecommunications networks is lacking. For instance, in Sub-Saharan Africa, over 60% of the population still lives without access to electricity, effectively severing them from the digital world. This infrastructural inadequacy hinders individuals' ability to participate in the digital economy, leaving them at a considerable disadvantage.

These infrastructural challenges are compounded by socio-economic factors that dictate individuals' ability to access digital technologies. Poverty remains a significant barrier, as low-income individuals are often unable to afford devices such as smartphones or computers, let alone the cost of internet services. A 2019 report by the International Telecommunication Union revealed that nearly half of the world's population is unable to afford internet access. This economic hurdle is exacerbated by the high cost of data in many parts of the world. In countries like Zimbabwe, data costs can exceed 20% of the average income, making regular internet use a prohibitive expense for most citizens.

A closer inspection of these barriers reveals a pronounced rural-urban divide. In urban areas, the availability of digital infrastructure and services is generally more developed, facilitating better access. Conversely, rural areas often lag significantly behind, with sparse infrastructure and fewer economic opportunities. This rural-urban divide is particularly evident in countries like India, where rapid urbanization has left rural areas grappling with inadequate infrastructure. In such settings, individuals face extreme challenges in accessing digital resources, widening the gap between urban and rural residents.

To illustrate these barriers in a tangible context, consider the case of rural schools in the Philippines. In many remote areas, schools struggle to provide even the most basic educational resources, let alone digital tools. Without proper internet access, students and teachers are cut off from a wealth of online educational content and tools that could significantly enhance learning. This digital disconnection perpetuates cycles of educational disadvantage, limiting students' potential and future opportunities. Initiatives like the "Tech4ED" program have sought to address these challenges by establishing community centers equipped with computers and internet access, empowering students and the broader community to engage with the digital world.

However, addressing these barriers requires not only technological solutions but also concerted policy efforts. Governments and international organizations have an important role to play in developing and implementing policies that address digital inequities. In some countries, ambitious public policies are making headway in this regard. For instance, Brazil's "Programa Nacional de Banda Larga" (National

Broadband Plan) aims to extend broadband access to underserved communities, with a particular focus on rural areas. The plan seeks to provide affordable and high-quality internet to boost economic opportunities and social inclusion, a testament to the power of targeted governmental intervention.

Furthermore, tackling the socio-economic barriers to digital access necessitates broader social policies that address underlying poverty and inequality. Efforts to make digital access more affordable can significantly impact underserved populations. For example, South Africa's "G-connect" project is one such initiative that provides free Wi-Fi in public spaces, making internet access more inclusive and equitable. By breaking down economic and infrastructural barriers, such programs can act as powerful catalysts for change, enabling individuals and communities to tap into the transformative power of digital technology.

In exploring the barriers to digital access, it becomes clear that the path to achieving digital equity is fraught with challenges and complexities. Yet, through dedicated efforts to address infrastructural inadequacies, socio-economic disparities, and rural-urban divides, significant progress can be made in bridging the digital gap. Recognizing that these barriers do not exist in isolation but are connected to broader socio-economic issues is crucial for crafting effective and sustainable solutions.

A practical example that underscores the impact of overcoming digital access barriers can be found in the efforts of Telecentre.org Foundation in Latin America. By establishing telecenters equipped with internet-connected computers and training programs, communities including displaced populations and marginalized groups have been able to access online learning, improve their employment prospects, and engage with broader social networks. These centers have become hubs of digital inclusion, demonstrating how targeted interventions can transform lives and communities by making digital access equitable and universal.

As we move forward in this exploration of digital equity, the lesson is clear: addressing the barriers to digital access requires a multi-layered approach that combines technological innovation with social and economic reforms. By understanding and dismantling these barriers, we pave the way toward a digitally inclusive future where everyone can participate fully in the digital age. With these foundational obstacles in perspective, we can now turn our attention to the myriad strategies that have been employed to foster digital equity and bridge these divides, as outlined in the next section of our discussion.

Subchapter 6.3: Strategies for Fostering Digital Equity

In our pursuit of a world where digital access is universally available, it becomes paramount to explore and understand the strategies that have been implemented successfully to foster digital equity. The disparity in digital access is not merely a technological issue but a profound social challenge that demands comprehensive and collaborative efforts. This subchapter delves into an array of approaches devised by governments, non-profit organizations, and the private sector, aimed at diminishing the digital divide and promoting a more equitable digital future. By examining these initiatives, we can glean insights into what works, how it can be scaled, and the potential roadmaps for regions still struggling with digital inequity.

Governmental Policies: Frameworks for Inclusive Connectivity

Governments across the globe have recognized the pivotal role they play in bridging the digital divide. Legislative measures and policies are being crafted to improve internet access and digital literacy, particularly in marginalized communities. For instance, Korea's "ICT Policy" has been notable for its extensive broadband coverage even in remote areas, making it one of the most connected countries in the world. Their focus on universal access through policy and infrastructure investment underscores the effectiveness of governmental intervention.

In another compelling instance, Finland became the first country to declare broadband internet access a legal right in 2009. This initiative was supported by clear policies that ensured broadband infrastructure reached the most remote corners of the country. The Finnish model stands as a testament to the potential impact of visionary governmental policies in nurturing digital equity.

However, policy needs to be coupled with practical execution. The United States' Federal Communications Commission (FCC) has embarked on the "Lifeline Program", which offers discounted phone and internet services to low-income consumers, helping bridge the access gap in economically disadvantaged areas. These examples illuminate the significance of governmental input not just in policy creation but also in facilitating real access and usage.

Nonprofit Interventions: Advancing Digital Literacy and Access

Nonprofit organizations have been instrumental in advancing digital equity, often reaching where governmental or commercial efforts fall short. Their grassroots initiatives can be transformative, as seen with India's "Digital Empowerment Foundation" (DEF). DEF has been a pioneering force in training populations in rural and underdeveloped areas to use digital tools, thereby enabling self-reliance in accessing information and service.

One of the standout projects is "Community Resource Centres" erected in Indian villages, where locals gain access to computers and the internet alongside guidance on how to utilize these resources effectively. This initiative demonstrates how localized, community-driven non-profit efforts can empower individuals and foster broader digital equity.

In Africa, organizations like "World Food Programme" have employed digital solutions such as cash transfer programs via mobile phones to ensure equitable food distribution, especially in regions with little to no traditional banking infrastructure. The crucial role of nonprofits lies in their ability to tailor digital interventions according to the nuanced needs of specific communities.

Private Sector Contributions: Corporate Social Responsibility and Innovation

The private sector, though often driven by profit, can contribute significantly towards digital equity through Corporate Social Responsibility (CSR) initiatives and innovative solutions. One prominent example is Google's "Project Loon", which aims to provide internet connectivity via high-altitude balloons to remote regions with minimal conventional infrastructure. This innovative approach illustrates the role of cutting-edge technology in surmounting traditional geographical barriers.

Moreover, Microsoft's "Airband Initiative" in the United States aims to bring high-speed internet access to rural areas by investing in new broadband infrastructure and leveraging innovative wireless technologies. This initiative not only brings connectivity but also reflects a sustainable business model whereby companies see long-term benefits from nurturing newly connected consumer bases.

A highlight in the corporate domain is IBM's "P-TECH" model, an educational initiative blending high school, college, and industry-recognized career paths in technology. By collaborating with educational institutions and businesses, this model seeks to create pathways to digital literacy and career readiness, indicating the interconnectedness of digital equity with employability and economic empowerment.

Case Study: The Success of Uruguay's "Plan Ceibal"

To elucidate the synthesis of these various strategies, consider Uruguay's ambitious "Plan Ceibal", an initiative launched with the aim of providing every child and teacher in the public education system with access to a computer. This program exemplifies multiple strategies that intersect at the core of digital equity: government policy, education, and technological advancement.

Since its inception, Plan Ceibal has distributed almost a million laptops, accompanied by extensive internet connectivity improvements at schools across the nation. The government has heavily supported this project, viewing it as an integral part of its educational policy. Educational elements are further fortified by the contribution of nonprofits and private organizations offering digital content and training aligned with the national curriculum.

Furthermore, Plan Ceibal transcends mere access to hardware, focusing on tutoring programs and workshops to develop digital skills among students and teachers alike. These efforts equip individuals with the competencies needed to navigate the digital realm effectively, thereby contributing to a cycle of long-term digital inclusion.

The broad outlines and impacts of Plan Ceibal serve to illustrate how a synergistic approach involving collaboration between governments, nonprofits, private companies, and the education sector can drive digital equity. By understanding and applying these multifaceted strategies, stakeholders globally can aim to replicate this success and chart similar paths towards fostering an inclusive digital future.

Summary and Transition

As these diverse strategies show, fostering digital equity is not a one-size-fits-all solution. It necessitates a delicate balance of policy, innovation, and localized action. The onus is on stakeholders from all sectors to recognize and act upon their roles in this expansive narrative sweeping our digital age.

Moving forward, the subsequent subchapter will explore the indispensable role of education in continuously bridging the digital gap. Education not only prepares individuals to engage with digital tools but also empowers communities on a broader level, creating a workforce better equipped for tomorrow's challenges. The next section will delve into educational initiatives that can further diminish disparities in digital access and literacy.

Subchapter 6.4: The Role of Education in Bridging the Digital Gap

In an increasingly digital world, the role of education in bridging the digital gap cannot be overstated. As we advance in our pursuit of digital equity, educational systems worldwide stand as crucial battlegrounds for implementing effective change. Education is the cornerstone upon which we can build a society equipped to handle the challenges and opportunities of the 21st century. In this subchapter, we will delve into how education can serve as a transformative force in narrowing the digital divide. We will explore how digital literacy and educational policies can empower underserved populations, analyze programs that integrate technology into learning, and discuss the pivotal role of educators in this process.

Digital Literacy: The New Essential Competency

Digital literacy is more than just the ability to use a computer or smartphone; it encompasses a range of skills required to navigate our digitally-connected world effectively. A digitally literate individual can critically evaluate information, understand digital tools, and participate in the digital economy.

With technology reshaping the job market, digital literacy has become as crucial as basic literacy and numeracy.

Governments and educational institutions must prioritize digital literacy from an early age. Countries like Estonia have set commendable examples with their robust digital education systems. Estonia implemented a comprehensive digital curriculum in all schools, ensuring students from a young age learn programming, data management, and cyber safety. This forward-thinking approach has not only fortified Estonia's digital economy but also minimized the digital divide within its population, showcasing education's potential to transform a society's digital landscape.

Moreover, digital literacy initiatives must not be confined to younger generations. Adult education programs play a pivotal role in upskilling older populations who may have missed out on early digital education. For instance, Singapore's "SkillsFuture" initiative offers learning credits for citizens, enabling them to take courses in digital skills, thereby ensuring all age groups can participate in and benefit from the digital economy.

Integrating Technology into Educational Curricula

Incorporating technology into educational curricula is another critical step toward bridging the digital gap. Merely having access to digital tools is not sufficient; students must engage with technology in a manner that enhances their learning experience and fosters critical thinking skills. Schools that integrate tablets, laptops, and other digital tools into their teaching can significantly enhance students' engagement and learning outcomes.

The "One Laptop Per Child" initiative, launched in several developing countries, is a prime example of utilizing technology to enhance education. By providing rugged educational devices to children in remote areas, this program aimed to offer an engaging and personalized learning experience. While challenges remain, such as infrastructure and teacher training, the program highlighted the potential of technology to offer educational pathways where traditional means fall short.

Furthermore, virtual classrooms and online courses have emerged as powerful tools in democratizing education. Platforms like Coursera, Khan Academy, and edX offer free or affordable courses from leading universities, making quality education accessible to anyone with internet access. Programs like these illustrate how technology can transcend geographical and financial barriers, enabling a broader audience to gain vital skills and knowledge.

Empowering Educators: The Linchpins of Digital Education

Central to integrating technology into education are the educators, they are the linchpins in ensuring a successful transition to a digitally inclusive future. Teachers must be adequately trained not only to use new technologies but also to integrate them effectively into their teaching. Therefore, investing in professional development for educators is crucial.

Finland provides an exemplary model in this regard. Finnish educators are extensively trained and given significant autonomy to implement digital tools as they see fit. This trust and investment in teachers have led to a highly skilled teaching workforce capable of creatively and effectively integrating technology into their classrooms. The result is an educational system where digital competencies are seamlessly interwoven with traditional skills, preparing students for a future that demands both.

Additionally, educators can be pivotal in driving community-wide digital literacy initiatives. By extending their reach beyond the classroom and into the broader community, teachers can lead workshops and courses that target parents and other community members. Such programs can not only enhance overall digital literacy but also foster a culture that promotes lifelong learning and adaptation to new digital realities.

Overcoming Challenges: Infrastructure and Policy

While digital education holds significant promise, myriad challenges persist, particularly in resource-limited settings. In many regions lacking basic infrastructure, establishing digital education can be daunting. Schools may lack electricity or internet connectivity, and even where these are present, devices may not be readily available. Thus, addressing infrastructure constraints is a fundamental step in making educational technology accessible to all.

Policy-making plays a critical role in this aspect. Governments must create and implement policies that prioritize investment in educational infrastructure, especially in rural and underserved areas. Successful case studies, such as India's Digital India initiative, demonstrate how policy-driven infrastructure development can support digital education. By focusing on expanding broadband connectivity and improving technological resources in schools, such initiatives aim to provide all students with access to digital education regardless of their location.

Furthermore, public-private partnerships can be pivotal in driving such initiatives. Collaborations between governments, technology companies, and educational institutions can mobilize the resources and expertise necessary to overcome infrastructure challenges. By working together, these entities can share the burden of cost and risk, accelerating the pace of digital transformation in education.

Case Study: Peru's Digital Leap

To illustrate the potential impact of integrating technology into education, consider Peru's recent digital initiatives. Recognizing the digital divide's profound impact on education, the Peruvian government launched a large-scale effort to integrate technology into its educational system. This program included providing digital devices to students and implementing teacher training programs focused on digital pedagogy.

Despite its economic constraints, Peru focused on rural areas, where the digital divide was starkest. By establishing internet connectivity and distributing tablets preloaded with educational content, Peru aimed to replicate the classroom experience in remote areas. Preliminary results suggest that these initiatives have improved student engagement and learning outcomes significantly, demonstrating that strategic investment in digital education can yield impressive returns even in resource-limited settings.

In summary, education serves as both a formidable weapon against the digital divide and a ladder lifting underserved populations toward better opportunities. As we equip schools, train educators, and develop policies that support digital education, we collectively forge a future where digital equity is not the exception but the norm. Transitioning to the next subchapter, we continue our journey by envisioning a digitally inclusive future and the multitude of possibilities it holds for economic and social advancement on a global scale.

Subchapter 6.5: Towards a Digitally Inclusive Future

As we turn our gaze towards a digitally inclusive future, the imperative of digital equity in shaping societal progress becomes undeniably evident. Digital access transcends mere connectivity, it embodies opportunities, rights, and human development. At this transformative crossroads, envisioning a future where digital equity is an integral societal infrastructure component requires an examination of collaborative pathways, innovative policies, and cultural shifts promoting digital inclusivity.

Embracing Collaboration Between Key Stakeholders

A digitally inclusive future hinges on collaborative efforts. Governments, corporations, non-profit organizations, educational institutions, and civil society each have a unique role in forming a digitally equitable world. Governments can spearhead policy-making and infrastructure development, ensuring affordable and widespread access to essential digital services. Key initiatives from policy-making bodies that prioritize investment in digital infrastructure can bolster nationwide connectivity. For instance, adopting nationwide digital policy frameworks such as the European Union's Digital Compass 2030, which aims to empower citizens with digital connectivity and skills, is a significant leap toward a digitally inclusive landscape.

Corporations, notably in technology and telecommunications, wield immense potential to influence digital access and equity. Through public-private partnerships and corporate social responsibility initiatives, businesses can extend their reach to underserved communities. A prime example is Google's Project Loon, which deployed high-altitude balloons in rural areas to provide internet access, bridging geographic gaps with innovative technology solutions.

Non-profit organizations can act as catalysts for digital literacy and community empowerment. By leveraging grassroots networks, they can deliver training and resources directly to those in need, using culturally appropriate methods to ensure inclusivity. The United Nations Children's Fund (UNICEF), through platforms like the Learning Passport, addresses educational gaps by providing digital access to educational content in remote areas.

Educational institutions are uniquely positioned to foster digital literacy. Schools can integrate digital competencies into their curricula, preparing students for the digital economy. A case in point is India's Digital India initiative, where schools have embraced information and communication technology (ICT) as a crucial component of education, equipping students with skills critical for navigating a digital world.

The Cultural Shift Towards Digital Inclusivity

Achieving digital inclusion requires a cultural shift that acknowledges the importance of digital rights as human rights. Societies must view internet access and digital literacy as essential, not optional. Public awareness campaigns to educate citizens about the significance of digital rights and inclusion can galvanize community support. For example, campaigns such as Digital4All have gained traction by emphasizing personal stories of transformation enabled by digital access, resonating with diverse audiences and highlighting inclusivity's power.

Moreover, digital platforms themselves must evolve in design and accessibility, reflecting inclusivity principles. Initiatives such as the Global Accessibility Awareness Day (GAAD) highlight the importance of accessible design across digital platforms, ensuring usability for all individuals, including those with disabilities.

Socio-Economic and Cultural Impacts of Digital Inclusion

The socio-economic benefits of digital inclusion are profound. Widespread digital access can drive economic growth by fostering innovation, entrepreneurship, and market expansion. Businesses with digital infrastructures can reach global markets, while digital platforms allow for remote working and learning, broadening employment opportunities. Economies that embrace digital transformation often witness increased efficiency, productivity, and competitiveness on the global stage.

Culturally, digital inclusion can facilitate social cohesion and broaden global perspectives. It allows diverse cultures to share their narratives and preserve their heritage digitally, ensuring representation in the broader digital dialogue. Instruments of cultural preservation like digital storytelling platforms enable communities to document their histories, arts, and cultural practices, fostering understanding and appreciation in a global context.

Practical Application: Case Study on Rwanda's Digital Journey

Rwanda, a nation that has emerged from historical challenges to become a beacon of digital progress, exemplifies the transformative impact of a commitment to digital inclusivity. Since the early 2000s, Rwanda has embarked on an ambitious plan to become Africa's ICT hub, prioritizing digital equity through policies and investments.

Through the National ICT Plan, Rwanda has integrated ICT into education, with initiatives like the "One Laptop per Child" program aimed at boosting digital literacy in primary schools. By collaborating with international partners, Rwanda has developed extensive fiber-optic networks that have revolutionized connectivity, especially in rural areas. This commitment has spurred entrepreneurship and innovation, with the emergence of tech startups positioning Rwanda as a leader in digital innovation on the continent.

Rwanda's story showcases how an unwavering commitment to digital inclusion, underpinned by strong governance, strategic partnerships, and investment, can transform a nation's trajectory. As the country continues to harness digital potential, it further solidifies its status as a model for digital equity.

Looking forward, this subchapter paves the way for the broader discourse on empowerment and connectivity in the subsequent sections of this book. The journey towards a digitally inclusive future invites reflection on individual and collective roles in advancing digital rights and access. Through sustained collaboration and innovation, the vision of universal digital inclusion becomes an attainable reality, heralding a world where digital equity serves as both a foundation and pathway to an empowered society.

As we close our exploration of digital equity and access, it is clear that the digital divide remains a formidable barrier to achieving universal digital inclusion, reflecting various economic, geographic, and educational disparities. We have uncovered the persistent barriers impeding digital access and highlighted successful strategies that demonstrate the power of collective effort in fostering digital equity. Education emerges as a transformative force, empowering underserved populations and equipping them with the skills necessary to thrive in the digital age.

The journey through this chapter underscores the urgency of bridging these digital gaps and the significance of strategic partnerships among governments, businesses, and nonprofit organizations. The diverse examples and case studies presented illustrate that change is indeed possible. They challenge us to envision a future where digital access is not a privilege but a basic human right.

The path to a digitally inclusive future is paved with collaborative initiatives and innovative solutions, inspiring us to play an active role in realizing this vision. By understanding the nuances of the digital divide and embracing strategies that promote equity, each of us has the potential to contribute to a more connected world.

As we turn towards the next chapter, we delve into how connectivity can empower individuals and communities, transforming digital access into a catalyst for social and economic development. Together, let us seize this opportunity to inspire change and drive progress in the digital era. Let the insights gained here propel you toward meaningful action, helping to construct a future where connectivity serves as a universal lifeline.

CHAPTER 7:
EMPOWERMENT
THROUGH
CONNECTIVITY

I n an era defined by the ceaseless exchange of information, the digital age has unraveled its most potent promise yet: empowerment through connectivity. As the world becomes increasingly interconnected, the internet emerges as a transformative catalyst, redefining how individuals and communities navigate life's complexities. This chapter, Empowerment through Connectivity, seeks to unravel the multifaceted ways digital connectivity serves as a bridge to empowerment, emphasizing its role as an instrument of individual strength and collective progress.

At the heart of this exploration lies the internet's fundamental capacity as an empowerment tool. The first section of this chapter delves into this profound capability, highlighting how digital access empowers individuals and societies alike by providing unprecedented access to information and networks. Through inspiring case studies, we witness firsthand how individuals, who might otherwise remain marginalized, surmount barriers and achieve personal and societal transformation.

The educational realm radically transforms under the lens of connectivity. Bridging Knowledge Gaps through Digital Access illustrates how digital platforms are revolutionizing education by democratizing knowledge. No longer confined by geography or financial constraints, learners can now access vast reservoirs of information and skill development opportunities. Through an array of narratives, this section underscores the internet's potential to make lifelong learning a reality for all, echoing the call for universal educational accessibility.

This chapter also ventures into the economic landscape, where digital connectivity acts as a vital engine for entrepreneurship and economic empowerment. Economic Opportunities and Digital Entrepreneurship presents vivid stories of innovation, where aspiring entrepreneurs harness online tools to establish businesses, reach distant markets, and uplift their communities. Through these narratives, we explore how digital connectivity can be a powerful force for economic growth, capable of lifting entire regions out of poverty.

However, empowerment through connectivity extends beyond individual achievements to encompass collective activism. Social Movements and Collective Empowerment explores the synergistic blend of digital connectivity and social justice, depicting how online platforms amplify marginalized voices and foster global solidarity. Through examples of digital activism, we witness how connectivity galvanizes social movements, empowering people to effect meaningful change and championing social justice from virtual spaces to tangible realities.

Despite its tremendous potential, the journey toward empowerment through connectivity is not without challenges. In the concluding section, Challenges and Opportunities in

Sustaining Empowerment, we delve into the barriers that threaten to undermine digital promise, such as digital literacy disparities, internet censorship, and the pervasive digital divide. Offering insight into strategies for overcoming these challenges, this section sets a forward-thinking groundwork for continued discussions on digital rights advocacy, ensuring that the empowering potential of connectivity is both sustained and inclusive.

In weaving together these threads, Chapter 7 serves as a beacon of insight into the empowering landscape of digital connectivity. It invites readers to ponder their roles in shaping a future where internet access is a universal right, a catalyst for equity, and a driver of societal transformation. As we embark on this exploration, may we be inspired to bridge divides, uplift voices, and harness the vast potential of connectivity to forge a more equitable and empowered world.

Subchapter 7.1: The Internet as an Empowerment Tool

In the unfolding story of the 21st century, the internet stands as a pivotal protagonist, offering unprecedented opportunities for empowerment to individuals and communities worldwide. Rooted in my experiences documenting digital transformation across diverse cultures, this subchapter delves into the critical role that digital connectivity plays in reshaping personal trajectories and communal structures. The internet's intrinsic ability to bridge distances and unite people through the flow of information, resources, and networks has marked it as a foundational tool for change. Here, we explore how this connectivity fosters empowerment at both individual and systemic levels.

The Internet as a Portal to Information

Information is often described as power, and in today's

world, access to information is primarily mediated through digital platforms. Historically, barriers such as geography, socio-economic conditions, and gender have limited access to information for many. However, the democratization of the internet presents a paradigm shift. By allowing instantaneous access to a vast repository of knowledge, it empowers people to make informed decisions, participate in civic life, and strive for economic and personal development.

Consider the story of Amina, a young girl from a rural village in Kenya. Growing up in a region where educational resources were scarce, Amina's prospects seemed limited. However, the introduction of a community-run internet center transformed her reality. Through online platforms, Amina gained access to educational content previously beyond her reach, from Khan Academy to free online textbooks. This digital access enabled Amina to excel in subjects that sparked her interest. Today, she is a software developer, working remotely for an international tech company, a testament to the transformative power of digital connectivity.

Networks and Communities: Building Collective Knowledge

Beyond individual empowerment, the internet serves as a crucial scaffold for building and strengthening communities. Digital networks provide platforms where individuals with shared interests and goals can convene, collaborate, and innovate. From professional networking sites like LinkedIn to niche online forums, the internet keeps ideas flowing and fosters a culture of collective growth.

One compelling example of this is the resurgence of indigenous languages through digital communities. In many parts of the world, indigenous languages are under threat, with cultural knowledge at risk of disappearing. However, online platforms have become vital spaces for speakers and learners to congregate, share resources, and cultivate communities focused on language revival. The Maori language in New Zealand, for instance, has seen a revival boosted by digital platforms where learners and native speakers interact regularly. Such communities highlight the internet's role as not merely a repository of knowledge but also a dynamic community-forming space.

Digital Advocacy and Self-Representation

A critical dimension of empowerment through the internet is the capacity for individuals and groups to represent themselves and their narratives authentically. This self-representation fosters dialogue and facilitates social change. Marginalized groups can bypass Gatekeepers who historically controlled media narratives and frame their own stories through blogs, social media, and other digital outlets.

Take, for example, the rise of the MeToo movement. What began as a hashtag quickly morphed into a global phenomenon, empowering countless individuals to share their experiences and demand systemic change. The movement underscored the internet's role as a catalyst for social activism, demonstrating its power to foster grassroots campaigns that challenge entrenched systems.

Overcoming Barriers with Digital Solutions

While the internet offers vast opportunities, significant barriers persist, holding back its full potential. Issues of digital literacy, access disparities, and variable internet speeds remain prevalent globally. Bridging these gaps is crucial to enabling meaningful empowerment.

A vivid portrayal of overcoming such barriers is visible in the story of rural entrepreneurs in Rajasthan, India. Supported by local NGOs, these entrepreneurs have harnessed digital tools to overcome market barriers inherent to their geographic isolation. By utilizing e-commerce platforms, they have successfully expanded their reach, marketing handcrafted goods internationally. Their journey emphasizes how strategic digital aid and community support can transform obstacles into opportunities.

The Pathway Forward: Empowerment through Connectivity

In our dynamic world, the empowerment potential of the internet continues to evolve, shaping interactions and societal frameworks. As we shift towards the next section on bridging knowledge gaps through digital access, it is crucial to recognize the internet's dual nature both as an enabler and a mirror reflecting existing inequalities. The stories of empowerment shared here not only highlight the optimistic potential of connectivity but also serve as a reminder of the challenges that must be tackled collaboratively. By considering the internet as an evolving tool, we can embrace its potential to empower more equitable, informed, and connected communities worldwide.

In conclusion, the practical application of these insights involves the ongoing development of sustainable digital strategies by policymakers, educators, and community leaders alike. A case study that exemplifies these principles is the "Internet Saathi" initiative in India, which embodies the vision of empowering rural women through digital literacy programs. By equipping women with smartphones and internet skills, they become community change agents, catalyzing learning and economic activity in their villages. Such initiatives remind us of the multilayered impact of digital empowerment, a theme that seamlessly ties into our subsequent exploration of bridging knowledge gaps through digital access, as we'll discuss in Subchapter 7.2.

Subchapter 7.2: Bridging Knowledge Gaps through Digital Access

Introduction to Digital Access and Knowledge Democratization

The advent of the internet and its proliferation as a readily available resource has fundamentally altered how knowledge is accessed and shared. Now, more than ever, digital connectivity serves as a beacon of hope for those seeking to overcome geographical, financial, or societal barriers in pursuit of education. This subchapter delves into the transformative power of digital access, illustrating its role in democratizing knowledge and empowering individuals across various spectrums of society.

Historically, educational opportunities were largely confined to individuals with access to formal schools and academic institutions. However, digital platforms have dismantled these age-old barriers, offering a myriad of resources online that cater to diverse learning needs. This democratization of knowledge holds particular significance in regions where traditional educational infrastructures may be lacking or inaccessible.

Digital Platforms and the Democratization of Education

Online Learning: The New Frontier

Educational technology has evolved beyond traditional e-learning models, with platforms such as Khan Academy, Coursera, Udacity, and edX leading the charge in global education reform. These platforms have curated high-quality courses from renowned institutions, making them available for anyone with an internet connection. This shift has facilitated the development of a more inclusive educational environment where individuals can tailor their learning experiences.

Consider the impact of initiatives such as Khan Academy, which provides free, world-class education to students worldwide. Sal Khan, founder of the academy, leveraged the power of video and interactive content to develop a robust learning ecosystem that reaches millions of students across different age groups and socio-economic backgrounds.

Another compelling example is Coursera, which partners with universities to offer courses ranging from basic literacy to specialized graduate-level subjects. By providing learners the ability to earn certified credentials online, Coursera has opened new avenues for professional advancement and skill acquisition.

Real-Life Case Study: A Story from Rural Kenya

In rural Kenya, electricity and internet connectivity can be scarce, but innovative local projects have brought change. A notable initiative is the installation of solar-powered Wi-Fi in remote communities, which has enabled students to access digital learning resources. One remarkable story is that of 15-year-old Wanjiku, who uses a tablet from her school's solar-powered hub to watch online lessons and prepare for exams. Through consistent access to resources that were once beyond her reach, Wanjiku has improved her academic performance significantly.

Overcoming Geographical and Economic Barriers

Breaking Barriers with Open Educational Resources

Open Educational Resources (OER) are another revolutionary facet of digital access. OERs refer to teaching, learning, and research materials that are freely available online for anyone to use, adapt, and redistribute. This approach to learning materials has dramatically reduced the cost of educational content, particularly beneficial for students in underfunded educational systems.

Projects like the Massachusetts Institute of Technology's OpenCourseWare (OCW) exemplify the impact of OER. By offering the institute's course materials online for free, MIT has empowered millions around the world to learn at their own pace, irrespective of their socioeconomic status.

Practical Application Example: OER in Action

Consider the case of a remote school in the Appalachian region. With limited budgets and a small library, access to MIT's OCW has allowed students to explore subjects beyond their curriculum, such as computer programming and environmental science. Teachers have incorporated these materials into their lessons, effectively broadening the scope of education offered in a resource-limited setting.

Promoting Lifelong Learning and Inclusivity

Digital Literacy and Lifelong Education

Beyond formal education, digital access serves as a conduit for lifelong learning, allowing individuals to continuously update their skills in a rapidly changing job market. Platforms like YouTube, TED Talks, and Google's Grow with Google offer a wealth of knowledge on diverse topics, from leadership skills to cooking techniques.

The internet's role in promoting lifelong learning is paramount in fostering an environment that values education at all stages of life. This transition towards a learning-oriented society reflects a broader commitment to inclusivity, ensuring that no one is left behind in the pursuit of knowledge.

Real-Life Scenario: Lifelong Learning for the Aging Population

In Estonia, the government has invested in digital literacy programs aimed at older adults. These programs provide internet access and training to elderly citizens, many of whom had minimal exposure to digital technology prior. For example, a retired teacher named Maie, at 68, learned to use online resources to engage with educational content relevant to her interests in history and biology. This newfound access has enriched her retirement years, highlighting the broad spectrum of opportunities lifelong learning presents through digital means.

Empowering Diverse Populations Through Collaborative Learning

Global Collaborative Platforms

Digital access doesn't just open doors for individual learning but also facilitates collaborative educational experiences. Platforms such as Google Workspace, Zoom, and Slack have redefined traditional group study dynamics, enabling students from different corners of the world to collaborate virtually on projects and share ideas.

These tools are particularly beneficial for fostering cultural exchange and understanding among students from diverse backgrounds. They provide a global stage for dialogue, allowing learners to connect and work together, regardless of distance.

Example of Global Collaboration: Virtual Cultural Exchange Program

A notable illustration of this concept is the partnership between a high school in Japan and one in Brazil. Through video conferencing tools and collaborative online platforms, students from both schools participate in cultural exchange projects. They work together on environmental science projects, sharing insights from their respective regions' ecosystems and conservation practices. This initiative not only enriches their academic understanding but also promotes intercultural empathy and collaboration skills.

Expanding the Horizons of Special Needs Education

Digital tools have also introduced groundbreaking changes in special needs education, providing customized resources that cater to individual learning requirements. Software applications utilizing voice recognition, text-to-speech, and interactive multimedia enable students with disabilities to engage with educational content effectively.

Assistive Technology in Special Needs Education

Take, for example, the TextHelp software suite, which supports students with dyslexia by providing reading and writing support tools. By allowing these students to access content through auditory rather than visual means, the software empowers them to participate fully in their learning environments.

Case Study: Inclusive Education in Action

A primary school in California implemented a pilot program using interactive educational software tailored for children with autism. The software facilitated learning through engaging visual and auditory prompts, accommodating different sensory preferences. Reports indicated an increase in students' engagement and learning outcomes, demonstrating the positive impact of digital access in special needs education.

The Role of Government and Policy in Digital Access

As the potential of digital access for education expands, governments across the globe are increasingly recognizing the need to enhance connectivity and digital infrastructure. Policies aimed at providing affordable internet access, upgrading digital equipment in schools, and training teachers in digital tools are critical to bridging knowledge gaps.

Governments as Catalysts for Education Reform

For instance, governments in countries like Singapore and Finland have implemented national strategies that provide robust ICT integration in education. These strategies include funding for technological advancements in educational institutions and ensuring nationwide high-speed internet access.

Practical Policy Example: Finland's Education Model

Finland's education model is renowned for its focus on equality and access to digital innovations. The Finnish government has prioritized technology in education by supporting initiatives aimed at developing digital literacy among teachers and students. Schools are equipped with state-of-the-art technology, ensuring that every student has an opportunity to engage with digital learning resources.

Challenges and Opportunities in Sustaining Educational Empowerment

While the benefits of digital access in education are evident, challenges such as the digital divide, cybersecurity risks, and technological biases pose significant hurdles. Persisting disparities in internet access and digital literacy can impede the equitable distribution of educational resources.

Addressing these challenges requires comprehensive strategies that involve stakeholders from public and private sectors. By advocating for universal internet access and equitable digital literacy programs, communities can work towards ensuring that the gains achieved through digital education are sustainable and far-reaching.

Transition to the Next Subchapter

As we explore the economic potential of digital connectivity in the next subchapter, it is essential to recognize that education is the cornerstone of economic growth. By equipping individuals with knowledge and skills, digital access lays the groundwork for a thriving digital entrepreneurship ecosystem.

Practical Application: Developing a Community Learning Hub

A compelling initiative has been the development of community learning hubs in underserved regions. These hubs offer free internet access, digital devices, and a library of educational content that community members can access. An example is the initiative by a non-profit organization in Bangladesh that created learning hubs in rural villages. These centers, powered by local partnerships, provide a safe and resourceful environment for community members to learn and thrive.

In conclusion, the journey through digital education is ongoing, and efforts to bridge knowledge gaps must be steadfast and inclusive. By laying the foundation for lifelong learning and education for all, digital access propels us toward a future brimming with possibilities. Let us now delve into the economic realm to explore how connectivity fosters entrepreneurship and innovation.

Subchapter 7.3: Economic Opportunities and Digital Entrepreneurship

The digital age has heralded a seismic shift in the way economic opportunities are created and pursued. At the heart of this transformation is the internet, a tool that has democratized access to information and resources, thus enabling economic empowerment and entrepreneurial ventures in unprecedented ways. This subchapter delves into the dynamic interplay between connectivity and economic growth, highlighting the innovative paths individuals and communities have taken to leverage online platforms for financial independence and wealth creation.

The Landscape of Digital Entrepreneurship

Digital entrepreneurship surpasses geographical constraints and has become a promising arena for innovation and economic development. For aspiring entrepreneurs, the internet offers a myriad of low-barrier entry points, including e-commerce platforms, digital marketing strategies, and social media reach, facilitating market access that was previously out of reach for those without substantial capital or network influence.

Consider the booming success of platforms such as Etsy and Shopify. These digital marketplaces have given artisans, creators, and small businesses around the globe a platform to showcase their products to a global audience. In regions where traditional retail infrastructure is lacking or prohibitively expensive, such platforms have been game-changers, enabling individuals to market their crafts and products beyond their local communities and into the global marketplace.

Empowering Women through Digital Means

The rise of digital entrepreneurship has been particularly empowering for women, many of whom face systemic barriers in traditional business environments. With the flexibility and accessibility provided by the internet, women can start and run businesses while managing other personal and familial responsibilities, thus enhancing their economic independence.

For instance, in rural India, the SEWA (Self-Employed Women's Association) initiative has empowered thousands of women by training them in digital literacy and entrepreneurship. Women involved in SEWA use smartphones and internet access to connect with markets, access vital information, and conduct mobile banking, which was previously inaccessible. This connectivity not only helps them increase their income but also paves the way for societal change by challenging gender roles and promoting gender equality.

Digital Tools and Economic Resilience

Digital tools have also enhanced economic resilience, particularly in underserved communities. During the COVID-19 pandemic, as physical businesses shuttered worldwide, many entrepreneurs pivoted online to sustain their livelihoods. For instance, in South Africa, small-scale farmers used WhatsApp to coordinate deliveries of fresh produce directly to customers, bypassing traditional market routes that were disrupted by the pandemic.

The global crisis highlighted the importance of digital platforms as safety nets and connectors during uncertain times. Those who had previously invested in digital literacy and tools were better equipped to navigate the crisis, demonstrating that digital preparedness can significantly contribute to economic resilience.

Access to Microfinance and Investment Opportunities

Microfinance institutions have also harnessed the power of digital connectivity to expand their reach and offer financial services to economically marginalized groups. These institutions leverage data and digital networks to extend credit and investment opportunities to individuals who lack traditional credit histories yet have viable business ideas. Platforms like Kiva and microfinance banks facilitate peer-to-peer lending wherein individuals from different parts of the world can invest small amounts in entrepreneurs across continents.

For example, in Southeast Asia, Gojek, an Indonesian ride-hailing, and payments company, has extended its services to finance small businesses, contributing to economic growth and job creation in the region. These initiatives demonstrate that with connectivity, financial inclusion is not just a possibility but a practical reality.

Education and Skill Development in the Digital Economy

Empowerment through connectivity also extends to skill acquisition. Online platforms such as Coursera, Udemy, and Khan Academy offer courses on entrepreneurship, digital marketing, coding, and more, often for free or at a low cost. For those with an entrepreneurial spirit but lacking formal education or resources, these platforms provide the necessary skills to succeed in the digital economy.

Take the example of Anwar Abdullahi, a refugee from Somalia who, through online courses, equipped himself with coding skills. Today, Anwar runs a successful web development firm from the Dadaab refugee camp in Kenya, serving international clients and providing employment for fellow refugees.

Challenges and Opportunities Ahead

While the internet's role in fostering economic opportunities is undeniable, challenges persist. Digital literacy remains a barrier for many, particularly in rural areas and developing countries. Additionally, access to affordable internet is not yet universal, exacerbating existing inequalities.

Furthermore, the digital market's hyper-competitive nature, data privacy concerns, and the threat of cybercrime are hurdles that digital entrepreneurs must navigate. Nonetheless, these challenges also provide opportunities for innovation and solutions that could drive further digital economic progress.

Case Study: The Rise of Agritech in Kenya

In rural Kenya, the rise of Agritech ventures exemplifies the transformative power of connectivity in agricultural communities. One notable success is the digital platform M-Farm, which allows farmers to access real-time market prices and sell their produce directly to buyers, thereby eliminating middlemen and increasing profits.

This platform, developed by local entrepreneurs, offers farmers an SMS-based service to compare prices and access new market links. By incorporating digital solutions into agriculture, M-Farm not only elevates farmers' incomes but also contributes to the broader national economy by fostering more robust agri-business ventures.

As this subchapter demonstrates, connectivity is a powerful enabler of economic opportunities and entrepreneurship. It opens doors for individuals and communities, providing tools and platforms to pursue financial independence and contribute to local and global economies. Moving forward, the challenge remains to broaden access and overcome the barriers that still exist, ensuring that the empowering potential of connectivity is universally realized. As we transition to the next section, we will explore how the internet has also evolved as a catalyst for social movements and collective empowerment, bringing a new dimension to global connectivity.

Subchapter 7.4: Social Movements and Collective Empowerment

In the expansive landscape of the digital age, the internet stands as a formidable catalyst for social movements and collective empowerment. As Dr. Eleanor Rees eloquently explores in this subchapter, digital connectivity serves as a dynamic conduit through which marginalized voices can surface, engage, and mobilize for social change. At the heart of this new paradigm is the democratization of activism, providing tools and platforms that transcend geographical boundaries, enabling individuals and groups to wield their digital presence as a lever for societal transformation.

Historically, initiating social movements required substantial resources, significant organizational capacity, and physical presence. Movements often relied on traditional media to disseminate their messages, limiting their reach to those who could attract media attention. However, the advent of the internet has revolutionized this space, creating a level playing field where emerging voices can initiate change from virtually any corner of the globe. This transformation is most evident in the various digital campaigns and online communities that have emerged over the past two decades.

The Virtual Spheres of Influence

Online platforms, such as social media networks, forums, and petition sites, have become digital agoras where discourse and activism intermingle. These platforms possess the unique ability to connect individuals with shared interests, fostering collective identity and purpose. In this virtual ecosystem, hashtags function as rallying cries, and videos become poignant narrators of untold stories. A prime illustration of this dynamic is the MeToo movement, which gained significant traction online, spearheading a global reckoning on sexual harassment and assault. Originating from a simple hashtag, it empowered a diverse cross-section of society to share personal experiences, generating a powerful narrative shift around issues of gender-based violence.

In many instances, these movements are born from informal networks of individuals who share common concerns. The accessibility of digital tools has democratized the capacity to document, share, and verify grievances, granting even the most disenfranchised a channel to the world. This accessibility represents an unparalleled opportunity for those in repressive regimes to bypass traditional media outlets and control their narrative. Platforms like Twitter and Facebook often emerge as critical tools when state-controlled media suppress dialogue, enabling activists to organize, communicate, and draw international attention to local issues.

Crafting Digital Campaigns

Crafting a digital campaign requires a nuanced understanding of the target audience, the issues at stake, and the medium's potential to disseminate messages. One of the core strategies involves engaging influencers and thought leaders who can amplify the reach of a movement. These figures often serve as catalysts, leveraging their platforms to spotlight causes and prompt widespread discussion.

A pioneering example is the climate advocacy journey of Greta

Thunberg. Her solitary protest outside the Swedish parliament became an international movement through strategic social media engagement. Greta's use of platforms like Twitter to chronicle her activism journey galvanized millions of young people worldwide, culminating in the global climate strike phenomenon. This case illustrates how digital campaigns, when orchestrated thoughtfully, can convert a lone voice into a global roar.

Engaging multimedia content is another powerful ally in the digital campaigner's arsenal. Videos, infographics, and podcasts can distill complex issues into digestible and emotionally resonant narratives. The visual documentation of incidents, such as police brutality or environmental degradation, can catalyze immediate emotional engagement, prompting swift action and rallying support.

Online Communities as Ecosystems of Change

Beyond campaigns, the internet has also spawned enduring online communities committed to sustained engagement and change. These communities operate as ecosystems of change, allowing individuals to exchange ideas, formulate strategies, and build networks of solidarity. Online forums dedicated to social causes often serve as incubators for innovative solutions, nurturing dialogue between activists, policymakers, and the general populace.

For instance, platforms like Reddit have given rise to subreddits focused on various social justice issues, providing spaces for open discourse, advice-sharing, and activism planning. The digital community r/BlackLivesMatter exemplifies this, where members not only discuss relevant topics but also coordinate activism efforts, such as protests and fundraising campaigns, to support the movement's goals.

Moreover, these online hubs often become the springboards for hybrid models of activism, blending physical and digital efforts to maximize impact. The 2019 Hong Kong protests highlighted how protestors used secure messaging apps like Telegram to organize and communicate, seamlessly pivoting between online coordination and real-world demonstration.

Digital Mutual Aid Networks

Another potent manifestation of digital connectivity is the rise of mutual aid networks. These decentralized groups utilize online platforms to coordinate and provide immediate, tangible support within communities. Unlike formal charity organizations, mutual aid networks emphasize reciprocity, collective responsibility, and solidarity rather than charity.

During the COVID-19 pandemic, a proliferation of digital mutual aid networks materialized globally, leveraging social media and community apps to collect and redistribute resources. These networks demonstrated the power of grassroots digital organization, highlighting how communities can rapidly respond to crises when equipped with connective technology.

A poignant case comes from the UK, where COVID-19 Mutual Aid UK, a network of local groups, utilized collaboration platforms like Slack and Facebook to connect thousands of volunteers with people in need. This grassroots effort provided essential support, such as grocery delivery and financial assistance, exemplifying the capacity for digital spaces to foster real-world resilience and empowerment.

Practical Example: The Arab Spring

An instructive exploration into the power of digital connectivity in social movements is the Arab Spring. This series of protests and uprisings swelled across the Middle East and North Africa between 2010 and 2012, largely ignited and fueled by digital activism. Social media platforms served as the oil in the engine of revolution, SPP social mobilization, calling for freedoms and governmental reforms.

In Egypt, for instance, platforms like Twitter and Facebook were instrumental in organizing the January 25th protests in Tahrir Square. Egyptians used these tools to mobilize, keeping the world abreast of their struggles in real time, thus applying international pressure on repressive regimes. Bloggers and citizen journalists, equipped with smartphones, chronicled events as they unfolded, circumventing state-controlled narratives and embodying a new paradigm of participatory media.

Real-life scenarios like these underscore the remarkable potential of connectivity to foster collective empowerment, catalyze social change, and lay the groundwork for unprecedented societal shifts. As we transition to the next subchapter, the focus will turn to addressing the inherent challenges and opportunities in sustaining this empowering potential of digital connectivity, laying out strategies for harnessing technology in a sustainable and equitable manner while considering the hurdles of digital literacy, internet censorship, and the pervasive digital divide.

Subchapter 7.5: Challenges and Opportunities in Sustaining Empowerment

As we traverse the landscape of digital empowerment, it is important to pause and consider the broader and sometimes nuanced challenges that come with sustaining the potential of digital connectivity. In an age where the internet is a lifeline for fostering education, entrepreneurship, and social change, the barriers that prevent full participation in the digital realm, such as digital literacy, internet censorship, and the digital divide, can hinder the equitable distribution of its benefits. Concurrently, opportunities abound for addressing these challenges, ensuring that the promise of the internet as a tool for empowerment continues to thrive and evolve.

Digital Literacy: A Fundamental Prerequisite

One of the preeminent challenges in harnessing the full potential of digital connectivity is the disparity in digital literacy across populations. Digital literacy extends beyond the ability to operate devices, it encompasses understanding how to effectively and responsibly use digital tools to access resources, communicate, and create content. In many communities, particularly those in underserved or remote areas, individuals lack the skills needed to navigate the digital world meaningfully.

For instance, consider a rural village in Kenya where access to the internet has recently been introduced. While the infrastructure may now support connectivity, the community members may not know how to harness this resource effectively. Nonprofits and educational programs have intervened in similar scenarios by providing workshops and training sessions designed to improve digital literacy. These initiatives are often run by local experts who understand the cultural context and can communicate effectively with the community. By equipping individuals with the skills needed to use the internet efficiently, such programs can unlock new avenues for education, business, and communication, thereby amplifying digital empowerment.

Internet Censorship: A Complex Barrier

Internet censorship poses another formidable barrier to digital empowerment, as it restricts access to information and stifles freedom of expression. In various parts of the world, governmental policies and regulations are put in place to monitor and control internet usage. These restrictions can prevent individuals and communities from accessing the global flow of information, effectively narrowing their view of the world and curtailing their opportunities for empowerment.

Despite these challenges, there are organizations dedicated to advocating for open internet access. The Open Technology Fund, for example, supports projects worldwide that aim to circumvent internet censorship and surveillance, empowering individuals to access unfettered information. Technological tools such as virtual private networks (VPNs) and digital privacy education have empowered users to bypass certain censorship measures, thus enabling a more open internet experience. Additionally, international pressure and diplomatic efforts can play a critical role in encouraging governments to adopt policies that align with global standards of freedom and transparency.

The Digital Divide: Equity in Connectivity

The digital divide remains one of the most pervasive challenges, often manifesting as disparities between those who have access to digital technologies and those who do not. Factors such as socioeconomic status, geography, and infrastructure development contribute to this divide, ultimately affecting the equitable spread of digital empowerment.

Efforts to bridge the digital divide are varied and multifaceted. Governments and international organizations invest in infrastructure to provide broadband access in remote and underserved areas, recognizing that connectivity is essential for participation in the modern economy. Meanwhile, private enterprises such as tech giants are developing low-cost technologies and platforms to increase access. For instance, Google's Loon project uses high-altitude balloons to deliver internet to remote regions, while SpaceX's Starlink initiative employs satellite technology to offer broadband internet access in hard-to-reach areas globally.

Opportunities for Sustainable Empowerment

While the challenges are significant, they also present distinct opportunities for creating sustainable empowerment through digital connectivity. Addressing these challenges requires a collective approach involving governments, private companies, non-governmental organizations, and local communities. By fostering collaboration, these entities can develop and implement policies, programs, and technologies that promote equitable access and digital literacy.

Educational institutions play a vital role in this endeavor, not only by integrating digital literacy into their curricula but also by partnering with technology companies to provide resources and training. Meanwhile, tech developers and entrepreneurs are encouraged to innovate with inclusivity in mind, ensuring that their products are accessible and affordable for diverse populations.

A notable example of a successful initiative is the collaboration between Microsoft and the United Nations Development Programme (UNDP) in Bangladesh. Together, they launched an ICT skills program aimed at empowering women with digital skills training. By equipping women with the necessary tools to navigate the digital realm, the program enhances their ability to participate in the local and global economy, thus contributing to societal growth and gender equality.

A Case Study: The Digital Empowerment Foundation in India

The digital landscape of India provides a compelling case study that illustrates both the challenges and opportunities in sustaining digital empowerment. India, with its vast population and diverse demographics, embodies a unique tapestry of digital connectivity that ranges from cutting-edge tech hubs to regions where basic internet access is a new reality.

The Digital Empowerment Foundation (DEF), an organization working extensively in India, exemplifies a successful model of addressing these issues. Established in 2002, DEF has been relentless in its mission to bridge the digital divide through innovative interventions and community-based programs. By setting up community information resource centers, DEF provides digital literacy education, access to e-governance services, and promotes digital entrepreneurship among rural populations.

One particular initiative that stands out is DEF's "Community Information Resource Centres" (CIRC) program, which transforms rural and underserved areas into digitally literate zones through access to technology and information. At the core of this initiative is the belief that community-driven solutions are vital for sustainable empowerment. For instance, CIRCs operate as hubs that facilitate interactions between local government services and citizens, thus making governance more transparent and participatory. Additionally, CIRCs offer localized content tailored to the specific needs and cultural contexts of the communities they serve, ensuring that digital literacy and empowerment are relevant and impactful.

By combining technology access with community-focused education and engagement, DEF not only equips individuals with essential digital skills but also fosters an environment where knowledge exchange and innovation can flourish. This empowerment enables community members to advocate for their rights, engage in civic responsibilities, and explore economic opportunities that were previously inaccessible.

A Call for Collective Action

As we turn the page on this chapter and look forward to exploring new dimensions of digital rights advocacy, it is clear that sustaining digital empowerment requires an ongoing commitment from all stakeholders. Digital connectivity is not just a tool, it is a cornerstone for building inclusive, equitable, and prosperous societies. The path ahead demands innovation, collaboration, and an unwavering dedication to ensuring that the empowering potential of the internet benefits every individual and community, regardless of geographical, socioeconomic, or cultural limitations.

Through continued exploration, storytelling, and advocacy, as exemplified in works by authors like Dr. Eleanor Rees, readers are encouraged to play an active role in shaping a digital future that values equity and sustainability. By doing so, we can forge connections that transcend boundaries and empower individuals to realize their full potential in this interconnected world.

As we progress, let us bear in mind that the journey towards sustained digital empowerment is an ongoing dialogue, a partnership between technology and humanity, consistently redefining what it means to connect, empower, and uplift the human experience.

As we draw the curtain on Chapter 7, we find ourselves immersed in the profound narrative of empowerment through connectivity. This chapter has traversed diverse landscapes, illuminating the internet's transformative power as an indispensable tool for individual upliftment and communal progress. We've explored how digital connectivity fosters access to vast reservoirs of information, dismantling barriers and offering new avenues for education, opportunity, and entrepreneurship. Through poignant case studies and inspiring narratives, we've seen how the internet bridges knowledge gaps, democratizes learning, and fuels economic independence, enabling individuals and communities to thrive.

Moreover, connectivity has emerged as a crucible for societal change, empowering social movements and amplifying marginalized voices to orchestrate meaningful action. Yet, as we celebrate these triumphs, we must remain vigilant of the challenges that persist. Issues such as digital literacy, censorship, and the enduring digital divide continue to threaten the sustainability of this empowerment. By confronting these challenges head-on, we can devise strategies that fortify the foundations of digital access, ensuring it remains a universal lifeline.

As we transition to the next chapter, we'll delve deeper into strategies for safeguarding digital rights, exploring policy frameworks and global initiatives that aim to extend the reach of connectivity even further. This journey invites us all to reflect on our roles as stewards of a digitally equitable future. Let us carry forward the lessons of empowerment, armed with the knowledge and determination to advocate for a world where the boundless possibilities of the digital age are accessible to all, propelling humanity toward a more just and connected future.

CHAPTER 8: THE ROLE OF GOVERNMENTS AND CORPORATIONS

As we stand on the precipice of a fully interconnected world, the threads that bind us are woven not just by technology itself, but by the aspirations and actions of human institutions committed to navigating this complexity. In Chapter 8, we delve into the dual-headed force of governments and corporations, entities wielding immense power and responsibility in shaping our digital lives. This chapter aims to illuminate the defining roles they play in advancing a digital landscape that champions universal access as a fundamental human right.

Historically, the quest for connectivity has been marked by milestones of progress steered by legislative vision and corporate ambition. However, these paths are not devoid of challenges, requiring an intricate dance of policy formation and tactical execution. Subchapter 8.1 sets the scene by scrutinizing the governmental stage, exploring how policies can either empower citizens with unprecedented access or falter, widening the chasm of the digital divide. Through case studies that span continents, we unravel the precise impact of governmental influence on the quality and reach of internet services, accentuating the necessity for strategic digital inclusivity.

The narrative then shifts in Subchapter 8.2, as we investigate the synergistic potential of public-private partnerships. These collaborations are emerging as vital engines of progress, striving to dismantle barriers to connectivity. We explore dynamic models where the ingenuity of the private sector complements the regulatory frameworks of governments, thus casting light on transformative approaches that redefine access for urban and rural landscapes alike.

Transitioning to the ethical sphere, Subchapter 8.3 positions corporate social responsibility (CSR) within the digital era. Here, we confront the imperative for corporations to extend their reach beyond profit and into societal impact, aligning business practices with the ethos of digital equity. Examining robust CSR initiatives, we uncover the significant role these efforts play in propelling internet literacy and inclusive technology use, narrowing the digital chasm one initiative at a time.

Economic considerations come to the forefront in Subchapter 8.4, where we dissect the implications of universal connectivity on global and local economies. Connectivity, as a catalyst, is juxtaposed with potential economic disparities that could emerge from its absence. By delving into economic data and trends, we underscore how digital infrastructure investments are not mere expenditures but vital contributors to sustainable economic ecosystems.

Finally, Subchapter 8.5 navigates the tightrope between regulation and innovation. This delicate balance is crucial; over-regulation risks smothering technological progress, while a laissez-faire approach endangers privacy and security. We explore how a judicious regulatory environment can foster innovation while safeguarding human rights, offering a blueprint for a thriving digital future.

In this chapter, we explore how these pivotal roles intersect and complement each other in the grand tapestry of digital rights. As we advance through the intricacies of policy, partnership, responsibility, economics, and regulation, the narrative not only addresses the present challenges but also envisages a collaborative future. Dr. Eleanor Rees calls upon her readers to imagine, and actively participate in, a world where digital opportunities are not a privilege but a promise, universally attainable and profoundly transformative.

Subchapter 8.1: Navigating the Digital Policy Landscape

The digital landscape of the 21st century is an intricate map of opportunities and challenges. At its core lies the essential role of governments in designing and implementing policies that promote digital rights and ensure universal access to the internet. As we navigate this terrain, one central question persists: How can governments construct effective digital policies that both advance accessibility and preserve the freedoms that a connected world should guarantee?

Governmental Influence on Digital Policy

Governments possess unparalleled influence in shaping the digital rights landscape, and their policy choices act as beacons guiding the path toward digital inclusion. In striving for universal access, governments often develop regulatory frameworks that can vary significantly in their success. Here, policy interventions can be seen as both gateways to progress and roadblocks when they fail to resonate with rapidly evolving technological environments.

A remarkable example of successful legislative intervention is found in Estonia. Known globally as a digital frontrunner, Estonia has leveraged its e-government initiatives to ensure comprehensive internet access for its citizens. These initiatives are driven by the nation's commitment to treating internet connectivity as a fundamental human right, showcasing the government's understanding of digital access as pivotal to civic participation and economic development. Through policies that provide every citizen with a digital identity and encourage public digital services, Estonia has simultaneously enhanced internet accessibility and increased societal inclusion.

On the other hand, the experiences of other regions illustrate the pitfalls of ineffective policy measures. Take, for instance, countries where legislation has lagged behind technological advancement, resulting in slow uptake of digital initiatives. In these scenarios, policies intended to regulate internet platforms or govern data privacy are often outdated by the time they are enacted, leading to gaps in coverage and a failure to protect users' rights in an ever-connected world.

Challenges in Policy Design and Implementation

Crafting effective digital policy requires a deep understanding of the socio-economic and cultural contexts unique to each country. It's not solely about the mechanics of technology or legislation but involves balancing diverse stakeholder interests and addressing potential inequalities in access and usage.

One of the universal challenges is managing the rapid pace of technology change versus the slower-moving gears of government legislation. As innovations such as 5G deployment, artificial intelligence, and blockchain gain traction, governments must move swiftly and knowledgeably to frame policies that harness the benefits of these technologies while safeguarding citizen rights.

Further, policy design is often inhibited by a lack of comprehensive data, which is essential for understanding citizens' needs and current levels of digital access. Without robust data, policies tend to be reactive rather than proactive, unable to anticipate future demands or mitigate potential inequalities in digital inclusion.

International Case Studies and Their Implications

To illustrate the diverse approaches and their impacts, we delve into a few key international case studies. In South Korea, the government's investment in digital infrastructure and its strategic push for internet penetration have served as a catalyst for the nation's tech-driven economy. The "IT839" strategy, for example, was a government initiative that targeted the development and convergence of internet infrastructure and services. As a result, South Korea now boasts one of the highest percentages of internet connectivity worldwide, widely credited with its role in fueling economic growth and innovation.

Contrastingly, in parts of Sub-Saharan Africa, efforts to increase connectivity have confronted barriers such as inadequate infrastructure and economic constraints. Yet, some countries within the region have begun investing in national broadband plans, driven by collaborative efforts with international organizations and tech conglomerates. These efforts focus on reducing entry costs and expanding infrastructure, emphasizing the necessity of a committed governmental approach in partnership with private enterprises to surmount the digital divide.

Governmental Obligations and Digital Inclusion

The exploration of policy failures underscores the obligation of governments to not only provide connectivity but to ensure equitable digital inclusion. This involves adopting an approach that goes beyond infrastructure deployment to encompass digital literacy training, equitable access, and fostering an environment where technological innovation benefits all societal sectors.

The dynamic between policy making and technological

advancement calls for governments to adopt adaptive policy-making strategies, an approach that involves continuous assessment and adjustment of policies to keep pace with technological innovations and socio-economic developments. For example, Iceland's open consultation processes involving public, private, and academic stakeholders in policy formation illustrate an iterative process that continually refines and adapts to technological changes and societal needs.

Practical Application: The European Union's Digital Agenda

To ground our discussion in a practical context, we turn to the European Union's Digital Agenda, launched as part of the Europe 2020 strategy. Its ambitious goals include promoting a digital single market, enhancing interoperability and standards, and fostering trust and security in the digital environment. This framework exemplifies a comprehensive policy approach encompassing not only accessibility but also broader economic and social dimensions.

A cornerstone of the Digital Agenda is the commitment to universal broadband coverage, demonstrated through initiatives like the Connecting Europe Facility that funds broadband projects across member states. The EU's approach emphasizes the integration of digital strategy within broader socio-economic planning, showcasing the potential of coherent regional policy to drive digital inclusion on a large scale.

Transition to Public-Private Partnerships for Connectivity

As we transition from exploring governmental roles, it becomes clear that addressing the digital divide requires an interconnected approach. In the subsequent subchapter, we will delve into the critical partnerships between public and private sectors as a means to enhance connectivity and implement the policies governments strive to enact. These partnerships present innovative models and frameworks to bridge technological gaps and drive meaningful progress toward universal internet access.

Subchapter 8.2: Public-Private Partnerships for Connectivity

In an era where universal internet access is increasingly seen as a fundamental component of modern life, innovative solutions are needed to extend connectivity to every corner of the globe. Public-Private Partnerships (PPPs) emerge as pivotal collaborative frameworks that leverage the strengths of both government institutions and private corporations. These partnerships can overcome significant barriers to internet access, addressing the digital divide that separates urban affluence from rural isolation and developed regions from developing areas.

Understanding Public-Private Partnerships

The essence of a successful PPP lies in its ability to combine public interest with private sector efficiency, technological advancement, and financial resources. Governments provide the regulatory frameworks and ensure that connectivity initiatives align with broader national strategies for digital inclusion. Meanwhile, private companies, particularly in the tech industry, contribute innovative technologies, expertise, and funding. The result is a mutually beneficial alliance that helps in deploying large-scale digital infrastructure projects.

Consider the role of regulatory frameworks established by governments. Without clear policies and legal pathways, private companies often face hurdles that inhibit infrastructure deployment. Conversely, governments sometimes lack the technological acumen or financial capacity to extend networks to underserved areas without risking public funds. Therefore, PPPs become the bridge, aligning invested interests with public returns through structured agreements.

Successful Models and Case Studies

Many countries have witnessed the transformative impact of PPPs in driving forward the connectivity agenda. In Kenya, for example, the government collaborated with Alphabet's subsidiary, Loon, to deploy balloon-powered internet in remote areas. As a nation with varied topography and large rural populations, traditional infrastructure approaches were insufficient for wide-scale connectivity. By utilizing high-altitude balloons equipped with internet transmitters, Loon was able to provide broad coverage, showcasing how companies can adapt technology for public benefit.

In India, the Digital India programme set an ambitious goal of universal internet access, particularly targeting rural connectivity. The government joined forces with private internet service providers and telecom companies such as Reliance Jio, which committed to investing heavily in 4G infrastructure. This collaboration has resulted in a dramatic increase in internet penetration, transforming the digital landscape across the country. Here, the state ensured policy support and eased regulatory pressures to create an enticing environment for corporate investment.

One cannot overlook the significance of Singapore's approach, encapsulated in the Intelligent Nation 2015 (iN2015) plan. By fostering partnerships between governmental bodies and telecom giants like Singtel, the initiative developed a high-speed Next Generation Nationwide Broadband Network. The project has placed Singapore among the top countries for internet speed and accessibility. This model exemplifies how a clear vision combined with active collaboration can bridge the divide and elevate a nation's digital presence.

Strategies and Best Practices

Beyond specific examples, best practices have emerged from these partnerships that are applicable globally. First and foremost is the importance of shared goals and objectives.

When both entities align on the desired outcomes, such as universal broadband, economic development, or technological advancement, the likelihood of success increases exponentially.

In addition, PPPs flourish when there is proper risk allocation: governments take on policy and regulatory risks, while corporations manage operational and market risks. This setup ensures that each party handles the areas where they excel, minimizing the chances of project failures or delays.

Clear communication channels and legal frameworks are also essential. Well-defined agreements that specify roles, responsibilities, accountability measures, and dispute resolution mechanisms aid in pre-empting conflicts and misunderstandings, ensuring the partnership is built on a foundation of trust and transparency.

Challenges and Considerations

Though PPPs present numerous advantages, they are not devoid of challenges. One significant hurdle can be the disparity in objectives between public and private sectors. Governments may prioritize equitable access, while corporations may focus on profitability and return on investment. Bridging this gap requires careful negotiation and incentive structuring, ensuring that both sides recognize the long-term benefits of widespread connectivity.

Additionally, maintaining equitable service provision in economically disadvantaged or hard-to-reach regions often necessitates financial models that may not be immediately profitable for private companies. In such cases, governments can implement funding mechanisms, like subsidies or tax incentives, to make projects more appealing for businesses.

Another concern with PPPs is ensuring that private interests do not overshadow public needs. Proper oversight and citizen engagement are vital in maintaining accountability, guaranteeing that the pursuit of profit does not compromise service quality or universal accessibility commitments.

Real-World Application: The Case of Rwanda

Rwanda stands as a dynamic case study of how a PPP can be leveraged to drive connectivity and digital transformation. The Rwandan government, in partnership with Korea Telecom, launched the 4G LTE network with the objective of covering 95% of the population. Recognizing the potential barriers, the partnership deployed not only physical infrastructure but also embarked on simultaneous digital literacy campaigns to maximize impact.

Through the collaboration, Rwanda saw a significant increase in internet users, and the development of a supportive digital ecosystem boosted local innovation and economic opportunities. By aligning interests and mutual benefits, Korea Telecom gained access to a burgeoning market, while Rwanda advanced towards its vision of becoming a regional tech hub.

Transition to Corporate Social Responsibility in the Digital Era

Public-Private Partnerships illuminate the power of cooperation in bridging the digital gap. However, achieving universal connectivity goes beyond infrastructural deployment; it encompasses the responsibilities of corporations to ensure this access is equitable and just. As we explore the next subchapter, we delve into Corporate Social Responsibility in the Digital Era, examining how businesses can embed digital inclusion into their ethos and operations for a thriving, connected society.

Subchapter 8.3: Corporate Social Responsibility in the Digital Era

In the past few decades, we've witnessed a tectonic shift in the role of corporations, particularly in the technology sector, as proponents of social change. As the gatekeepers to digital access and facilitators of digital literacy, these corporations bear an ethical responsibility to ensure that their actions contribute positively to the digital landscape. This subchapter delves into the multifaceted realm of Corporate Social Responsibility (CSR) in the digital era, exploring how companies can align their business models with the principles of digital equity and inclusive growth.

The Evolution of CSR in the Digital Space

Traditionally, the concept of CSR focused on environmental conservation, philanthropy, and ethical labor practices. However, in this digital age, the focus has expanded to include digital rights and internet access. Companies are now called upon not just to operate responsibly, but to actively participate in bridging the digital divide through targeted CSR initiatives.

Global tech giants like Google, Microsoft, and Facebook have illustrated innovative CSR approaches aimed at enhancing digital inclusion. By tapping into their extensive resources and technological prowess, these corporations are not only addressing connectivity but also promoting internet literacy, which is crucial for making the digital world accessible to all.

Aligning Business Models with Digital Equity

Fostering digital equity is not just an ethical mandate; it is increasingly recognized as a strategic business move. Companies that integrate digital equity into their core business strategies are likely to expand their market reach, drive consumer loyalty, and build sustainable models of growth. For instance, by investing in community-based internet projects, a company can simultaneously nurture a future customer base while promoting societal welfare.

Salesforce, a leader in cloud-based software, has demonstrated this model through its 1-1-1 philanthropic model, dedicating 1 percent of its equity, product, and employee time to improve communities around the world. This approach has catalyzed digital literacy programs in underserved areas, enhancing local capacities to utilize the digital tools that are increasingly indispensable for personal and professional growth.

Case Studies of Effective CSR Initiatives

1. Google's Project Loon: Innovation in CSR can be seen through initiatives like Google's Project Loon, which aims to provide internet access to remote areas via high-altitude balloons. The project's pilot, conducted in Indonesia and Sri Lanka, has shown promising results in making internet connectivity not only feasible but sustainable even in challenging terrains. By doing so, Google not only boosts its brand image but also fosters an internet-empowered populace that may later utilize Google's services, thus reinforcing its market position in these regions.

2. Cisco Networking Academy: Launched in 1997, Cisco's Networking Academy is another excellent example of CSR in action. This program offers IT skills training that helps individuals to develop skills necessary for digital careers. Serving over 12,000 educational institutions across 180 countries, the academy stands as a testament to the power of education as a tool for empowering equitable digital access. By fostering a skilled workforce, Cisco ensures a steady supply of talent capable of driving innovation in the IT sector.

3. Facebook's Express Wi-Fi: Facebook's Express Wi-Fi is an initiative aimed at improving connectivity in areas with poor internet access. By partnering with local entrepreneurs to provide low-cost internet services, the initiative strengthens local economic conditions while enhancing digital equity. This relational element not only helps local businesses thrive but also promotes wide-scale usage of Facebook's platform and services.

Strategies for Narrowing the Digital Divide

To successfully implement CSR initiatives that narrow the

digital divide, companies must adopt multifaceted strategies:

- Partnership Programs: Collaborating with NGOs, governmental bodies, and other corporations can amplify CSR efforts. Partnerships with local organizations ensure that initiatives are culturally sensitive and appropriately targeted.

- Investment in Education: Committing to educational initiatives that raise awareness about digital careers and promote internet literacy can have a far-reaching impact. This includes setting up scholarships, sponsoring open-source educational platforms, or providing tech mentorship programs that equip individuals with essential digital skills.

- Infrastructure Development: Companies can invest in developing robust digital infrastructure in regions that lack connectivity, such as installing broadband networks, supporting community internet centers, and investing in technology hubs.

- Proactive Policy Engagement: Corporations can leverage their influence to support policy changes that facilitate digital inclusion. Advocacy and lobbying for inclusive regulations can ensure enduring systemic change.

Real-Life Scenario for Application

Imagine a small village in sub-Saharan Africa, untouched by the strides of the digital revolution. The residents rely heavily on traditional agriculture, and their connectivity is limited to sporadic mobile signals. Recognizing this gap, a leading tech company initiates a CSR project, collaborating with local partners to establish a community tech hub powered by solar energy. This hub not only provides internet access but also serves as a center for digital education, where residents can learn skills from basic internet navigation to advanced coding.

As time passes, the knowledge gained from the hub propels locals to launch digital enterprises, craft cooperatives market their products online, farmers employ digital platforms to optimize their yield, and students attend virtual classes. The community witnesses significant socioeconomic upliftment, setting an example and encouraging replication in nearby regions.

By crafting CSR initiatives that resonate at the community level, corporations can transform isolated locales into digitally empowered societies. This goal aligns seamlessly with the larger mission of digital inclusivity and presents a roadmap for ongoing efforts in the public-private sphere, as discussed in subsequent sections of this chapter. The next subchapter will delve into the economic implications of fostering universal connectivity, integrating perspectives on how these social responsibilities yield mutual benefits for economies at large.

Subchapter 8.4: Economic Implications of Universal Connectivity

In the current epoch of rapid digitization, the concept of universal internet access transcends mere convenience; it is a linchpin of economic vitality. As technological interdependence deepens across industries, the internet serves as an infrastructure of opportunity unparalleled in modern economics. Universal connectivity catalyzes economic growth, spurs innovation, and underpins sustainable development. Conversely, the absence of connectivity contributes to economic fragmentation, widening inequality, and lost opportunities. Herein, we dissect the economic dynamics fostered by universal connectivity and explore the challenges inherent in this transformative paradigm shift.

1. Economic Growth through Connectivity

A connected society is an economically empowered society. Access to the internet facilitates the flow of information, triggering a cascade of economic activities. For instance, small businesses operating in remote areas gain access to broader markets online, amplifying their reach and profitability. By democratizing access to information, connectivity fosters entrepreneurial activity, subsequently driving job creation.

A study by the World Bank found that a 10 percent increase in broadband penetration can lead to a 1.38 percent increase in a developing country's GDP. This correlation underscores the transformative power of the internet as an economic equalizer. Countries with higher internet penetration often experience accelerated economic growth, with a marked increase in GDP per capita.

2. Innovation as a Byproduct of Connectivity

The internet is a breeding ground for innovation, acting as a crucible for ideas that can redefine industries. The startup ecosystems in technologically advanced countries vividly illustrate this phenomenon. Silicon Valley, for instance, flourishes as a cradle of innovation significantly due to its pervasive connectivity and digital infrastructure.

Innovation not only thrives in well-resourced environments but also finds fertile ground in unlikely places. Consider the proliferation of mobile payment systems in Sub-Saharan Africa, regionally adapted solutions like M-Pesa have transformed the local economy by providing financial services to underserved populations, prompting significant shifts in economic behavior and empowerment.

3. Challenges and Economic Risks of Connectivity Gaps

Despite its potential, the digital divide remains a monumental barrier to economic cohesion. Geographic, socioeconomic, and demographic factors contribute to persistent connectivity gaps that stymie economic growth. The lack of infrastructure in remote or rural areas, high costs of internet access, and insufficient digital literacy fundamentally limit economic participation in the digital age.

The economic ramifications of these gaps are significant. Disconnected regions face challenges in competing in the global market, leading to systemic inequalities. For instance, agricultural producers in isolated areas may fail to access the latest market data, affecting their ability to make informed decisions. Similarly, lack of internet access limits educational opportunities, constraining the potential workforce talent pool and stifling future innovation.

4. Strategic Investments in Digital Infrastructure

Bridging these gaps necessitates strategic investments in digital infrastructure, which must be prioritized as national economic strategies. A robust digital foundation can attract international investments, spur technology transfer, and integrate countries into global value chains.

Countries like Estonia have emerged as exemplars of digital investment, creating e-Estonia, a countrywide initiative that embraces digital inclusion as a national ethos. By investing in nationwide digital infrastructure, Estonia has equipped its citizens with e-residency, digital voting, and comprehensive online public services, fostering an environment ripe for economic agility and growth.

5. Public and Private Sector Roles in Economic Advancement

Collaboration between governments and corporations is essential in building the infrastructure necessary for universal connectivity. Corporations can bring technological expertise and innovation, while governments can establish conducive regulatory environments and ensure equitable access. Initiatives such as Alphabet's Project Loon, which deploys high-altitude balloons to deliver internet to remote regions, illustrate the creative solutions arising from such collaborations.

Moreover, public policies should incentivize private sector investments in digital infrastructure, providing tax breaks or subsidies for projects that enhance connectivity. Governments can also consider regulatory measures that ensure fair access to essential internet services, avoiding monopolistic practices that inflate costs and restrict access.

6. Connectivity and Economic Resilience

The COVID-19 pandemic starkly highlighted the economic resilience provided by digital connectivity. Businesses that could pivot to online models weathered the storm more effectively than those that relied solely on in-person interactions. The capacity to participate in digital commerce, remote work, and online education has become integral to economic stability in our globally connected ecosystem.

In India, the rapid growth of digital payment systems like Paytm during the pandemic showcased the resilience facilitated by digital solutions. With nationwide lockdowns in place, businesses relied on these platforms to sustain their operations, demonstrating how digital infrastructure can enhance economic resilience in times of crisis.

7. Harnessing Connectivity for Sustainable Development

Universal connectivity holds the promise of aligning economic growth with sustainable development. As we evaluate the potential for digital solutions to promote environmental sustainability, we find that connectivity can reduce carbon footprints, for example, through the facilitation of remote work and digital conferencing.

By supporting digital agriculture initiatives, connectivity can also contribute to sustainable economic practices. The use of satellite data and IoT technologies in agriculture allows for precision farming techniques that optimize resource use and increase crop yields with minimal environmental impact.

8. Practical Application: Kenya's Digital Transformation

As a practical illustration of these concepts, let us consider Kenya, a country that has leveraged connectivity to drive economic transformation through digital innovation. Kenya's mobile money platform, M-Pesa, not only revolutionized financial services but also stimulated a broader range of economic activities. By enabling easy money transfers and access to credit for previously unbanked populations, M-Pesa fostered entrepreneurship, increased financial inclusion, and stimulated economic growth.

Additionally, the Kenyan government's investment in digital initiatives like Konza Technopolis, a technology city designed to propel the country's move towards a digital economy, further emphasizes the economic potential rooted in increased connectivity. This initiative aims to create a business hub that attracts IT businesses and fosters job creation, showcasing how strategic investment in digital infrastructure can catalyze economic development.

As we transition to Subchapter 8.5, we delve further into exploring how a delicate balancing act between regulation and innovation shapes the future of our digital societies. The symbiotic roles of governments and corporations are complex, yet pivotal, in facilitating a landscape where economic expansion via connectivity is both equitable and sustainable.

Subchapter 8.5: Balancing Regulation and Innovation

In the dawn of the digital age, societies around the globe have encountered a persistent and dynamic challenge: striking an ideal balance between regulation and innovation. As we stand on the brink of an era where technological advancements redefine human interactions, governments and corporations grapple with the formidable task of nurturing innovation while ensuring the protection of fundamental rights. The complexity of maintaining this equilibrium is not merely a matter of policy but a deeply nuanced exploration of societal values, technological capabilities, and economic imperatives.

This subchapter embarks on an in-depth examination of the intricacies involved in balancing regulation and innovation, highlighting the pivotal roles institutions play in shaping our digital futures.

The Dual Role of Regulation

Regulation traditionally serves as a mechanism to ensure safety, security, and ethical practices within societal frameworks. Governments, while functioning as regulators, aim to construct infrastructures that safeguard public interests, prevent malpractices, and foster equitable growth. However, they concurrently face the critical task of crafting policies that do not hinder technological innovation.

Historical Context of Regulatory Impact

History provides numerous instances where regulation has elicited both positive and adverse outcomes on innovation. The 1980s U.S. telecommunications deregulation is often cited as a catalyst for innovation. By relaxing existing constraints, it enabled a competitive marketplace that spurred advancements in communication technology. In contrast, the stringent patent laws applied to the biopharmaceutical industry underscore a regulatory approach that, while intended to protect investments in research, has at times stifled more rapid innovation due to extended monopolistic periods limiting generic medication production.

Modern Regulatory Challenges

In the current digital era, the stakes are considerably higher. Technologies like artificial intelligence, blockchain, and Internet of Things (IoT) present unprecedented potential alongside new regulatory challenges. Issues of privacy, data protection, and cybersecurity sit at the forefront of regulatory agendas. In instances where regulation is overly restrictive, such as the European Union's General Data Protection Regulation (GDPR), the intended protections can extend to inadvertently stalling data-driven innovation by imposing significant compliance burdens.

Conversely, lightly regulated sectors, such as the initial years of cryptocurrency markets, often demonstrate how lack of regulatory frameworks can invite activities like fraud, financial instability, and consumer exploitation.

The Role of Corporations in Innovation

Corporations, as pioneers of technological advancements, possess a profound influence over both market trends and regulatory landscapes. Their inclination towards agile methodologies and rapid implementation of innovative ideas shapes how new technologies interface with society.

Self-Regulation and Ethical Pioneering

Tech giants, by nature of their global influence and resources, often navigate regulatory terrains more adeptly and innovatively than smaller entities. Self-regulation and ethical frameworks established by companies can mitigate potential over-regulation by governments. Google's AI Principles and Microsoft's Committee on AI and Ethics serve as exemplary practices of corporations taking proactive steps to address ethical concerns surrounding technology development.

Corporations also play a central role in lobbying for regulations that are conducive to continued innovation. Their engagement with policymakers helps align industry goals with regulatory intentions, ensuring mutually beneficial outcomes.

Global Case Studies on Regulatory Balance

A practical discourse on regulation and innovation would be incomplete without examining case studies highlighting successful global approaches:

Singapore's Agile Regulations

Singapore's dynamic regulatory environment exemplifies an agile governance model, offering regulatory sandboxes that enable technology companies to test innovations within controlled conditions before a full-scale release. This approach, particularly in fintech, has bolstered innovation while simultaneously establishing robust consumer protection.

Singapore's Infocomm Media Development Authority (IMDA) actively collaborates with industry stakeholders, demonstrating a proactive approach to policy that encourages innovation without sacrificing safety and ethical standards.

The Nordic Model in Sustainability

In Scandinavia, budding green technologies due to robust governmental support and relaxed regulatory frameworks have resulted in unprecedented growth in sustainable innovations. Here, regulative measures have not only kept pace with technology but have also anticipated market needs, primarily through collaborative policymaking between governmental bodies and private innovators.

Pathways for Developing Balanced Policies

To forge policies that achieve balance, governments and corporations must pursue collaborative engagements, seek cross-border consensus, and emphasize consumer-centric policies.

Innovation Hubs and Cross-Sector Collaboration

Governments can create innovation hubs, bringing together academia, industry, and regulators to stimulate collaborative development and preemptive problem-solving. An example is Israel's high-tech innovation landscape, where government policies actively facilitate research and development, yielding a thriving environment for tech startups.

Fostering Transparency and Accountability

Data transparency remains foundational in ensuring accountability within both regulatory and corporate spheres. Establishing open channels for reporting regulation impacts can provide governments with real-time feedback to adjust regulations that might inhibit technological growth excessively.

Developing Flexible Regulatory Frameworks

Adopting flexible frameworks allows regulations to evolve alongside technological advancements. Legislative bodies can incorporate sunset clauses and rolling reviews, ensuring that outdated regulations do not burden the tech ecosystems or hinder innovative trajectories.

Practical Application: The Case of Europe's AI Policy Framework

The European Union's evolving strategy for AI regulation provides a telling example of balancing regulation and innovation. Built on a foundation of ethical AI guidelines, the EU aims to establish itself as a global leader in trustworthy AI. By prioritizing human rights, safety, and privacy, while also fostering AI advancements, the EU's policy framework stands as a testament to the possibilities of harmonizing regulatory imperatives with innovation's demands.

This strategy reflects an understanding that the decisive role of government should not merely be control, but facilitation, harmonizing protective measures with mechanisms that propel technological excellence.

Balancing regulation and innovation is not an endpoint but a continued endeavor, a narrative porcelain of governance and creativity. As we adapt to this rapidly shifting landscape, we embrace the potential for technology to harmonize with society's ethical foundations, ensuring a digital future where progress resonates with the core of human rights and prosperity.

As we conclude Chapter 8, we recognize that the quest for universal internet access hinges on the intertwined efforts of governments and corporations. By elucidating the complexities of digital policy landscapes, successful public-private partnerships, corporate social responsibility, economic implications of connectivity, and the crucial balance between regulation and innovation, this chapter lays a robust foundation for advancing digital rights.

For governments, the path forward involves crafting inclusive policies that genuinely enhance digital access and quality, setting the stage for a more connected society. Meanwhile, corporations have an ethical mandate to align their operations with the ideals of digital equity, leveraging their influence to extend internet literacy and access. Together, these entities must navigate the delicate dance between aiding innovation and ensuring citizen rights, always pursuing a future where connectivity serves as an equalizer rather than a divider.

Reflecting on these core takeaways, you as readers are invited to consider your role, whether as policymakers, business leaders, or informed citizens, in championing the cause of digital inclusion. Imagine the transformative potential of a world where every individual can harness the power of the internet as a tool for learning, economic opportunity, and personal empowerment. Your engagement is vital in advocating for policies and practices that bridge the digital divide.

As we transition to the next chapter, we will delve deeper into the human stories and societal impacts of digital transformation. We will explore the cultural shifts and the nuanced narrative of digital empowerment, continuing our journey toward a vision where connectivity becomes a universal lifeline. Stay with us as we unfold the possibilities of a future fortified by inclusive digital rights, advancing our collective human freedom in the digital age.

CHAPTER 9: VOICES FROM THE FRONTIER

Welcome to the digital frontier, where the complex tapestry of digital rights comes alive through a chorus of diverse voices. In Chapter 9, aptly titled "Voices from the Frontier," we embark on a journey to explore the multifaceted dialogue surrounding digital rights in an era where technology proliferates at an unprecedented pace. As our digital world expands, so too must our understanding and approach to the rights and responsibilities it entails.

Setting the stage in Subchapter 9.1, we delve into the vibrant sphere of diverse perspectives, where the discourse on digital rights is illuminated by insights from various disciplines, including technology, law, sociology, and education. This section underscores the significance of drawing from a wellspring of expert viewpoints to fully grasp the challenges and opportunities that digital rights present. By incorporating a broad spectrum of perspectives, we aim to construct a nuanced and comprehensive understanding of what it means to protect and promote digital human rights.

The journey continues in Subchapter 9.2, where we examine the societal impacts of digital technology. Digital advancements are not merely technical enhancements; they are social engines, reshaping norms and interactions. Here, we explore how digital rights influence societal frameworks, touching on democratic practices, cultural exchanges, and social movements. This section brings to light the transformative power of technology to create more inclusive landscapes, while also confronting the critical issue of digital exclusion and the invisibility of marginalized voices.

In Subchapter 9.3, we delve into the ethical and moral terrain of connectedness. The widespread reach of digital connectivity brings forth a complex ethical landscape, raising questions about data privacy, online surveillance, and algorithmic bias. Through the lens of digital ethics, we reflect on the duties of individuals, corporations, and governments to uphold ethical standards. By engaging with these topics, we pave the way for informed policy-making and advocate for enhanced digital literacy.

Next, in Subchapter 9.4, we navigate through the innovations and challenges at the digital frontier. Emerging technologies like artificial intelligence and blockchain promise to reshape the future of digital rights. We discuss their potential to empower individuals, while also addressing the risks they pose, such as exacerbating digital disparities and complicating governance frameworks. This exploration encourages readers to consider strategic avenues for leveraging technological advancements to advance equitable digital rights for all.

Finally, Subchapter 9.5 presents a rallying call for building a collective vision for digital freedom. Synthesizing the insights gathered, we underscore the need for collaboration across sectors and communities to achieve digital freedom. By highlighting global success stories and cooperative efforts, this section envisions a future where stakeholders unite to advocate for common goals, setting the tone for subsequent discussions on future-oriented strategies for digital rights.

In "Voices from the Frontier," we invite you to engage with the evolving narratives that define digital rights, urging a collective reflection on our role in shaping an inclusive digital future. Together, let us chart a path where connectivity becomes a universal lifeline, empowering societies to thrive in harmony with technology.

Subchapter 9.1: Diverse Perspectives on Digital Rights

In the daunting complexity of today's digital world, the concept of digital rights has emerged as a pivotal debate, traversing beyond mere accessibility and into the realms of ethics, law, and social equity. As humanity finds itself increasingly reliant on the interconnected web of technology, understanding digital rights requires more than a cursory glance; it demands a kaleidoscope of voices and disciplines. Dr. Eleanor Rees, in her characteristic investigative narrative, unpacks these diverse perspectives with a deft hand, grounding the discourse in a rich tapestry of insights and experiences from across global spheres.

Understanding the Digital Rights Landscape

The discourse surrounding digital rights is richly layered, involving a spectrum of considerations from privacy to freedom of expression, data security to equitable access. To holistically engage with such a multifaceted issue, interdisciplinary perspectives are indispensable. Here, experts from fields including technology, law, sociology, and education become instrumental in piecing together a comprehensive picture. Each field provides a unique lens: technology experts illuminate the practicalities of digital implementation; legal scholars navigate the frameworks that uphold these rights; sociologists explore the social ramifications; educators advocate for knowledge dissemination and literacy.

Consider the debate on data privacy, a cornerstone of digital rights. Technologists might focus on encryption and secure data handling processes, ensuring privacy through innovation. Lawyers, on the other hand, dissect regulatory frameworks such as the General Data Protection Regulation (GDPR) to safeguard personal data, ensuring that digital interactions are legally sound. Meanwhile, sociologists may consider the societal impacts of data usage, examining how data breaches might affect trust in digital systems. Teachers and educators promote digital literacy, ensuring individuals understand how to protect their data and navigate online spaces safely.

In recounting these processes, Dr. Rees draws on real-world scenarios, such as the implementation of privacy laws across different jurisdictions, emphasizing how diverse perspectives not only enhance understanding but also forge pathways to compromise and innovation.

The Intersection of Technology and Law

For a more nuanced understanding, it's essential to delve deeper into the intersection of technology and law, a critical nexus in the digital rights discourse. As digital technologies advance at a staggering pace, legal systems often struggle to keep pace, grappling with unprecedented challenges. Consider, for example, the rise of artificial intelligence and its implications for privacy and surveillance. Legal and technological domains must work in concert to ensure that these advancements contribute positively to society.

Dr. Rees cites the European Union's efforts to regulate AI through comprehensive policy proposals as a potent illustration of interdisciplinary collaboration. The EU's legislation aims not only to protect citizens' rights but also to encourage technological innovation, striking a delicate balance. Similarly, the United States, with its Federal Trade Commission's guidelines, seeks to manage corporate handling of AI while leaving room for technological growth. These regional efforts, though varied, contribute to a global dialogue, prompting further interdisciplinary research and collaboration.

Sociological Insights and Digital Justice

Turning to sociology, one must consider the digital divide, a pressing issue that highlights the disparities in access to technology and the internet. While connectivity has become a staple in urban landscapes, rural and underserved populations remain marginally connected, if at all. This divide perpetuates inequality, affecting education, economic opportunities, and social mobility. Dr. Rees brings attention to stories from around the globe: communities in Sub-Saharan Africa where mobile networks are scarce, or rural areas in the United States where high-speed internet is still a luxury.

She recounts the experiences of children in rural India who climb to hilltops to access online educational resources, illustrating the profound implications of digital exclusion. Here, the sociological perspective emphasizes the urgency of bridging this divide, shining a spotlight on grassroots movements and initiatives striving to provide equitable access. Collaboration between governments, NGOs, and tech companies has begun to yield promising results, but the road towards total inclusivity remains fraught with challenges.

Educational Strategies for Digital Literacy

In the educational sphere, digital literacy is paramount. Understanding one's rights and responsibilities in the digital realm empowers individuals to navigate it safely. Dr. Rees articulates this notion through case studies of schools that integrate digital literacy into their curricula. In Finland, for instance, where digital education is a compulsory element of the curriculum, students learn not only how to use digital tools but also to critically analyze online content, understanding the ethical implications of their digital actions.

Educational institutions play a vital role in driving awareness and understanding of digital rights. However, Dr. Rees acknowledges that educational efforts must extend beyond schools, encompassing lifelong learning and community education programs to reach adults and disadvantaged groups. In exploring initiatives in countries like Brazil, where community centers provide free digital literacy workshops, the narrative shifts towards empowering individuals, ensuring that everyone can participate in the digital economy.

Collaborative Synergies: Technology and Social Activism

Social activism finds fertile ground in the digital age, where online platforms become powerful tools for advocacy and change. Dr. Rees chronicles movements such as the Arab Spring or the more recent Black Lives Matter protests, where digital connectivity amplified voices and mobilized action globally. The landscape of activism is now inextricably tied to digital rights, freedom of speech, access to information, and the ability to assemble virtually become cardinal rights in modern activism.

This interplay between technology and social activism exemplifies the transformative potential of digital connectedness. Yet, it also warns of the inherent risks: online censorship, misinformation, and digital repression by authoritative regimes. This intricate dance underscores the importance of ongoing dialogue and collaboration among technologists, activists, and policymakers to safeguard digital freedoms while curbing misuse.

Practical Case Study: From Theory to Application

To underline the confluence of these perspectives, let us consider Estonia, a beacon in digital transformation. This small Baltic state has championed digital rights through its comprehensive e-governance model, facilitating unparalleled access to digital services for its citizens. From online voting to e-health records, Estonia's digital society reflects a collaborative endeavor, drawing on technology, law, and education to empower citizens.

Technologists designed a secure digital ID system, pairing innovation with robust legal frameworks to ensure security and trust. Educators have implemented widespread digital literacy programs, ensuring that the population remains informed and engaged. This comprehensive approach has not only advanced digital rights but also fostered a more participatory and transparent democracy, setting a precedent for others to follow.

Transition to Societal Impacts of Digital Technology

As we journey from the foundation of diverse perspectives, the immediate question becomes: how do these digital rights shape our societies? In the subsequent subchapter, we delve into the societal impacts brought forth by digital technology, exploring how this complex weave of rights and innovations redefines our communal and global interactions. Through an examination of social norms and digital movements, we will elucidate how digital rights transition from abstract concepts to tangible societal transformations. Join us in uncovering the transformative narrative of technology as it crafts more inclusive and expressive societies.

Subchapter 9.2: Societal Impacts of Digital Technology

In the vibrant streets of New Delhi, a young entrepreneur uses social media platforms to kickstart a movement for educational reform. Simultaneously, halfway across the world, a small village in rural Kenya gains worldwide attention through a viral video advocating for clean water access. These scenarios illustrate the transformative power of digital technology in reshaping societal norms and interactions, a phenomenon that is swiftly unfolding across the globe. As we unpack the impact of digital rights on social structures, we observe a nuanced and multifaceted evolution of how communities engage, express, and advocate.

Redefining Democratic Practices

Digital technology serves as a catalyst that reinvigorates democratic practices. By enabling real-time communication and allowing voices once silenced by geography or circumstance to be heard, digital platforms have fundamentally altered the political landscape. For instance, consider how platforms like Twitter have amplified the reach and impact of the MeToo movement. This campaign, which started online, mobilized millions globally to share their experiences with sexual harassment and assault, leading to significant policy changes and greater public awareness.

Moreover, digital initiatives such as e-governance platforms have redefined citizen engagement with governments. Estonia's digital identity program, for instance, offers citizens unfettered access to government services, from voting to accessing healthcare. This level of interaction not only streamlines processes but also fortifies the democratic ideals of transparency, accountability, and participation.

Cultural Exchanges and Borderless Interactions

The digital realm transcends geographical boundaries, facilitating cultural exchanges unprecedented in previous eras. Online platforms allow individuals from disparate corners of the world to share stories, art, and ideas, creating a vibrant tapestry of global dialogue. The influence of South Korean pop culture, or "Hallyu," is a testament to this borderless interaction. Through platforms like YouTube and Spotify, K-pop and Korean dramas have garnered a massive international following, enriching cultural diversity and understanding worldwide.

However, this accessibility also introduces challenges. The

dominance of a few powerful platforms risks homogenizing cultural expressions, potentially overshadowing local cultures. Balancing a diverse digital landscape demands conscious efforts to preserve and promote indigenous and minority voices, aligning with the ethos of digital rights by ensuring equitable representation in digital spaces.

Social Movements and Digital Advocacy

The proliferation of social media and digital tools has revolutionized how social movements are organized and sustained. Movements such as the Arab Spring and Black Lives Matter exemplify how digital technology aids grassroots advocacy, allowing activists to mobilize rapidly and efficiently. These platforms facilitate coordination, resources sharing, and global visibility, effectively amplifying voices that might otherwise remain unheard.

Take, for example, the Standing Rock Sioux Tribe's protest against the Dakota Access Pipeline. Through the strategic use of digital platforms, the protest gained international support and media attention, highlighting indigenous rights issues to a global audience. This digital camaraderie underscores the potential of technology to galvanize support and drive change.

However, the digital sphere is not without its limitations and pitfalls. Movements can face digital censorship, misinformation spreads rapidly, and the physical-digital divide can exclude marginalized communities from fully participating in these dialogues. Addressing these issues is paramount to maintaining the integrity and inclusivity of digital advocacy.

Digital Exclusion and the Invisibility of Marginalized Communities

Despite the transformative power of digital technology, digital exclusion remains a formidable barrier. As digital platforms become integral to social, economic, and political participation, those without access are invariably left behind. The digital divide is not just about connectivity but also encompasses digital literacy, affordability, and relevance.

In many low-income communities around the world, limited internet access inhibits opportunities for education, employment, and civic engagement. In rural Africa, for instance, internet penetration remains low compared to urban areas, exacerbating existing socio-economic disparities. To combat this inequity, initiatives such as Facebook's Internet.org aim to bring free basic internet services to underserved regions, although such ventures raise concerns about net neutrality and corporate control over information access.

A case study of interest is India's Digital Village initiative, which seeks to empower rural areas through comprehensive digital connectivity, focusing on local entrepreneurship and e-education. This initiative demonstrates the potential of targeted digital inclusion programs to bridge gaps and foster community development.

Integrative Solutions for Digital Equity

Creating a more equitable digital landscape requires concerted efforts from governments, corporations, and civil society to collaboratively address digital exclusion and promote equal opportunities for all. Digital literacy initiatives can equip individuals with the skills necessary to navigate the digital world, essential not only for personal empowerment but also for societal participation.

Governments can enact policies that incentivize infrastructure investment in underserved areas, while corporations can pursue inclusive business models that balance profit with social impact. Importantly, platforms must foster environments that are welcoming to diverse voices, cultivating algorithms that avoid bias and promote fairness.

Practical Application: Case Study of Kenya's M-Pesa

A compelling case study illustrating the societal impact of digital technology is Kenya's mobile banking system, M-Pesa. Emerged initially as a mobile money transfer service, M-Pesa has redefined economic participation and enterprise in the region. By providing financial services to individuals without traditional banking access, it has significantly increased financial inclusion in Kenyan society.

The implications of such a transformative tool extend beyond financial inclusion. M-Pesa users have reported improvements in overall well-being, with increased access to education and healthcare facilitated by financial stability. Moreover, the success of M-Pesa has inspired similar models worldwide, highlighting the potential of digital solutions to address systemic issues.

This exploration of digital technology's societal impacts underscores the importance of digital rights as a foundation for inclusive, equitable participation in our increasingly connected world. As Dr. Rees transitions into exploring the ethical and moral dimensions of digital interconnectedness, it is crucial to keep examining how these impacts align with our values and responsibilities in nurturing a digital society that benefits all.

Subchapter 9.3: Ethical and Moral Implications of Connectedness

In the digitally interconnected world we inhabit today, discussions around digital rights are inextricably linked to complex ethical and moral considerations. As we stand on the precipice of increasing digital integration, this subchapter delves deep into these ethical landscapes, illuminating the diverse and often challenging questions that arise when digital connectivity becomes ubiquitous.

Data Privacy and Personal Autonomy

At the core of digital ethical debates lies the issue of data privacy, a fundamental aspect of personal autonomy in the digital realm. In an era where data has been heralded as the new oil, its management, protection, and ethical utilization have become critical concerns. Personal data, spanning from browsing habits to intimate health information, is continuously collected by corporations and governments under the guise of providing better services or enhancing national security.

Consider the case of Cambridge Analytica, which exemplified the dark side of data utilization. By harvesting data from millions of social media profiles without explicit consent, this firm manipulated user information to influence voter behavior, highlighting the critical issue of consent and control over personal data. Such instances illuminate the urgent need for stringent data protection laws that respect individual privacy and ensure transparency in data handling, a need echoed in public discourse and regulatory responses, such as Europe's General Data Protection Regulation (GDPR).

The intricacies of data privacy also encompass issues of surveillance. In many regions, omnipresent surveillance systems have created digital panopticons that infringe upon privacy. This pervasive monitoring, often justified by national security, challenges individuals' rights to freedom from unwarranted observation, raising the question of how society balances safety with liberty.

Algorithmic Bias and Fairness

As algorithms increasingly govern aspects of our daily lives, from news feeds to credit scoring and beyond, ethical challenges surrounding bias and fairness have taken center stage. Algorithms, while seemingly objective, often inherit biases present in their training data. This can lead to discriminatory practices that disproportionately affect marginalized communities.

A striking example is the use of algorithmic decision-making in the criminal justice system. In the United States, some jurisdictions employ predictive policing tools that have been criticized for reinforcing racial biases. These systems, trained on historical crime data, can inadvertently perpetuate existing social inequities, resulting in over-policing of communities of color.

Addressing algorithmic bias requires transparency in algorithm development and rigorous ethical evaluations to ensure fairness and equity. Initiatives such as the Algorithmic Justice League have emerged, advocating for accountability in algorithmic design and deployment. Moreover, fostering diversity in the teams developing these technologies is crucial to mitigating biased outcomes and crafting systems that reflect a broader spectrum of human experience.

The Responsibilities of Stakeholders

Navigating the ethical thickets of digital connectedness necessitates a multi-stakeholder approach, where individuals, corporations, and governments share the responsibility of upholding ethical standards.

For individuals, digital literacy encompasses not just technical skills but an understanding of digital rights and responsibilities. Educating users about the implications of their digital footprint, data rights, and privacy measures can empower them to make informed decisions and advocate for their rights online.

Corporations wielding significant technological power bear the burden of ethical stewardship. Beyond profitability, companies must prioritize ethical considerations in their operations, ensuring that the technologies they develop do not exploit or harm users. Mechanisms for corporate accountability, like public transparency reports and independent ethical reviews, can help ensure responsible business practices.

Governments, too, play an essential role in upholding digital rights through policy frameworks, regulation, and international cooperation. They are tasked with negotiating the delicate balance between innovation and regulation, ensuring that technological progress does not outpace ethical considerations. Cross-border collaborations to address global cyber challenges, alongside domestic policy adaptations, are paramount to fostering a fair and equitable digital ecosystem.

Practical Application: A Case Study in Digital Ethics Education

To underscore the real-world applicability of these ethical considerations, let us examine a pioneering initiative in digital ethics education. The University of California, Berkeley, has launched a comprehensive course titled "Ethical and Social Issues in Technology," aimed at equipping students across disciplines with the tools to tackle ethical challenges in technology.

This course encourages students to explore the implications of emerging technologies through case studies, role-playing exercises, and debates. By examining real-world scenarios, such as data breaches and AI biases, students develop the ability to critically assess the ethical dimensions of technology. This approach not only enriches their understanding but also prepares a new generation of leaders who can navigate the complex moral landscapes of our digital future.

As we transition to the next exploration of innovations and challenges at the digital frontier, it becomes apparent that understanding these ethical dimensions is not solely an intellectual exercise. Instead, it is a foundational pillar for shaping a future where digital rights are harmoniously integrated into the fabric of our global society, preparing us for the imminent technological advancements ahead.

Subchapter 9.4: Innovations and Challenges at the Digital Frontier

In the dawning era of digital transformation, innovation and challenge move in a delicate dance, each step echoing across landscapes of opportunity and uncertainty. This subchapter explores the pivotal roles of emergent technologies at the digital frontier, spotlighting how they both bolster and challenge the realization of equitable digital rights. From artificial intelligence to blockchain, each technological advancement carries the potential to reshape the contours of digital empowerment while simultaneously surfacing new complexities in governance and ethical considerations.

Emerging Technologies Shaping the Future

At the forefront of digital innovation is artificial intelligence (AI), a technology that harnesses vast amounts of data to drive sophisticated decision-making solutions. AI's ability to process information at unprecedented speeds and accuracy can vastly improve access to information and services. For example, in healthcare, AI algorithms can analyze medical images more accurately than human counterparts, enhancing diagnoses and patient care. This digital advancement democratizes access to high-quality medical advice, a cornerstone of digital rights.

However, AI's influence extends beyond its potential benefits. Concerns regarding algorithmic bias and discrimination highlight a significant challenge at the digital frontier. When AI systems are trained on data that reflects societal biases, they can perpetuate or even exacerbate inequalities. This problem is particularly acute when considering digital rights for marginalized communities. A 2019 study conducted by the AI Now Institute found that facial recognition systems demonstrated significant racial bias, misidentifying individuals of different ethnicities at higher rates. Such instances underscore the need for transparent, fair, and accountable AI systems to protect against digital rights violations.

Blockchain technology, another trailblazer, promises to revolutionize how digital identities and transactions are managed. With its characteristic decentralized and immutable ledger system, blockchain promises enhanced security and privacy. In countries with unstable governance or weak institutions, blockchain could provide a robust framework for protecting personal data and ensuring transparency in public records, thus promoting digital empowerment.

Yet, blockchain is not without its hurdles. Its implementation requires significant computational resources and energy consumption, contributing to environmental concerns. Additionally, the decentralized nature of blockchain poses regulatory challenges, making it difficult for governments to control or issue guidance, potentially leading to legal and financial ambiguities.

Digital Empowerment vs. Digital Divide

The promise of digital technologies lies in their potential to empower individuals by providing equitable access to information, services, and opportunities. The growth of the Internet of Things (IoT), connecting devices and enabling sophisticated data exchange, exemplifies how digital societies can be more interconnected than ever before. Consider the impact of smart city initiatives, where IoT devices improve efficiencies in public transport, energy consumption, and urban planning, leading to enhanced quality of life.

Despite these advancements, the digital divide remains a pervasive issue. Access to digital technologies is not evenly distributed, with vast disparities between urban and rural areas, developed and developing countries, and among different socioeconomic groups. For instance, in rural India, despite the increase in mobile phone usage, access to high-speed internet remains sporadic and unreliable, thereby excluding millions from the benefits of digital participation.

This divide is not limited to physical access to devices or the internet; it also encompasses digital literacy. The ability to effectively navigate, understand, and utilize digital tools is foundational to exercising digital rights, yet many educational systems are ill-equipped to teach these essential skills, leaving populations behind as the digital revolution marches on.

The Governance and Regulation Conundrum

The rapid advancement of digital technologies necessitates a reevaluation of governance structures. Traditional regulatory frameworks often struggle to keep pace with technological innovation, creating a gap that risks compromising digital rights. Governments around the world grapple with how to balance innovation with protection, ensuring that new technologies contribute positively to societal well-being.

A poignant example is the European Union's General Data Protection Regulation (GDPR), a landmark attempt to safeguard personal data in the age of digital connectivity. By setting stringent data protection requirements, the GDPR seeks to give individuals more control over their personal information. However, implementing such comprehensive regulations poses significant challenges, especially for smaller companies that may lack the resources to fully comply, potentially stifling innovation.

Moreover, regulatory measures must navigate the transnational nature of digital technologies. The internet's borderless realm often conflicts with national regulations, creating a complex legal environment where digital rights can be easily compromised.

The Path Forward: Harmonizing Innovation and Rights

As digital technologies continue to evolve, the pursuit of

equitable digital rights becomes ever more critical. To bridge the gap between innovation and regulation, collaborative efforts across governments, civil society, and the private sector are essential. Multi-stakeholder approaches can ensure that diverse voices contribute to shaping a digital landscape that promotes rights and empowerment universally.

Education plays an indispensable role in this endeavor. Promoting digital literacy programs can equip individuals with the skills necessary to participate fully in the digital world, turning digital divide into digital empowerment. Also, fostering ethical development practices among technology developers and companies is essential for mitigating biases and ensuring that technological advances reflect the true diversity of the societies they serve.

Practical Application: The Case of Estonia

To illustrate the potential of harmonizing digital innovation with rights, consider Estonia, often lauded as a digital society pioneer. Following its independence from the Soviet Union, Estonia invested heavily in technology infrastructure, considering internet access a fundamental right for its citizens. The country implemented e-Estonia, an innovative digital ecosystem that enables citizens to access public services online, vote electronically, and manage personal data securely through a digital identity system.

Estonia's commitment to digital empowerment has facilitated significant societal advancements. It set an example of how strategic investment in digital technologies can advance societal goals and enhance digital rights. However, Estonia's approach also highlights the importance of addressing cybersecurity challenges and ensuring that data privacy remains central to digital governance.

As technology continues its relentless march forward, the pathways explored and challenges encountered by Estonia serve as a beacon of possibility for a world navigating the digital horizon. This interplay of innovation, rights, and governance establishes a bedrock from which future strategies can be built, inviting broader dialogues on digital freedom as we transition into Subchapter 9.5: Building a Collective Vision for Digital Freedom.

Subchapter 9.5: Building a Collective Vision for Digital Freedom

In our quest for digital freedom, we stand at a pivotal juncture where the intersection of technology, human rights, and collective activism can sculpt a new paradigm for connectivity. This subchapter delves into the intricate process of constructing a unified vision that propels digital rights forward, emphasizing the power of collaboration across sectors. Guided by the insightful narratives and principles of Dr. Eleanor Rees, we explore how diverse stakeholders can converge to advocate for a digital future that is both inclusive and empowering.

The Framework for Collaborative Advocacy

To build a cohesive vision for digital freedom, it is imperative to establish a framework that brings together disparate voices from various sectors, technology, law, academia, civil society, and governance. Each sector contributes unique insights and expertise, forming a comprehensive tapestry of strategies essential for tackling the multifaceted challenges of digital rights.

Technology plays a crucial role by setting the foundation for advancements through innovations such as open-source software, which democratizes access and allows individuals to participate in digital creation without barriers. Organizations like Mozilla have led the way by not only developing platforms that are open and accessible but also by advocating for internet health and privacy as fundamental rights.

Legal frameworks underpin digital rights, ensuring they are recognized as basic human rights. The General Data Protection Regulation (GDPR) in the European Union serves as a robust example of legislation that prioritizes user privacy and data protection, empowering individuals against unwarranted surveillance and data exploitation. Such legislation highlights the importance of enforceable rights and the pivotal role of policymakers in championing these causes.

Academic institutions and researchers contribute by studying the impacts and implications of digital technologies on society, often providing empirical data and theoretical insights that inform policy and technological development. Collaborative projects between universities and tech corporations, like those seen in initiatives spearheaded by MIT, foster innovative approaches to tackling digital inequality.

Civil society groups are vital in amplifying the voices of marginalized communities, ensuring that efforts towards digital rights do not overlook those often left in the shadows of technological progress. Nonprofits and grassroots movements, such as Access Now, utilize digital tools to mobilize support and hold governments accountable for human rights transgressions in the cyberspace.

Lastly, governments have the capacity to bridge digital divides by investing in infrastructure that ensures connectivity reaches remote and underserved areas. Efforts like South Korea's National Information Society Agency illustrate how state-led initiatives can drastically improve internet access and literacy, thereby enhancing digital participation across populations.

Success Stories and Global Initiatives

The journey towards digital freedom is replete with inspiring stories of successful collaborations that offer valuable lessons for collective action. In India, the Digital India initiative serves to unite various sectors in a mission to empower citizens through technology. The program focuses on improving online infrastructure, expanding connectivity, and enhancing citizens' digital literacy, demonstrating the transformative potential of governmental commitment to digital rights.

Meanwhile, international organizations such as the United Nations have recognized the significance of internet access as a part of sustainable development, placing digital connectivity on the global agenda. The UN's Roadmap for Digital Cooperation underscores the importance of global partnerships in promoting a "universal, open, and inclusive" internet that facilitates human development.

Another exemplary model is the collaboration between local communities and international tech companies in Africa, aimed at lowering connectivity barriers through innovative uses of technology. Google's Project Loon and Facebook's internet.org (now Free Basics) have attempted to leapfrog traditional infrastructure challenges by providing internet via aerial balloons and satellite technology, although these solutions have also sparked debate over data control and privacy.

Challenges in Forging a Unified Vision

While these success stories illuminate pathways forward, the journey is not without obstacles. Disparities in technological access across regions and communities exacerbate existing social inequalities, creating a dual-speed digital landscape where some advance rapidly while others are left behind. Additionally, ideological differences about surveillance, privacy, and the role of state versus corporate governance in digital spaces can fragment efforts towards a universal digital rights framework.

Diverse entities must navigate these challenges by fostering open dialogue and negotiation, striving to balance innovation with ethical considerations. Understanding cultural contexts and respecting local norms are crucial in crafting policies and technologies that align with the diverse needs of global populations.

Practical Application: A Case Study in Community-Led Connectivity

To ground these discussions in practical application, let us examine a case study from rural Kenya, where community-led initiatives are making strides in bridging the digital divide. The case of the Tunapanda Institute illustrates how grassroots efforts can achieve remarkable progress in digital literacy and connectivity.

Tunapanda Institute, a tech and media education nonprofit based in Nairobi, empowers youth from marginalized communities by offering free training in digital skills, entrepreneurship, and creative technology. Through a collaborative model, the institute partners with local businesses, international nonprofits, and government entities to bring technology and education to areas traditionally excluded from digital opportunities.

This partnership has resulted in the establishment of community-based digital hubs, where access to the internet and digital tools facilitates learning and innovation. The hubs serve as incubators for local talent, enabling participants to launch startups, contribute to the tech ecosystem, and effect social change in their communities.

By adopting a participatory approach to digital education, the Tunapanda Institute not only equips individuals with practical skills but also fosters a sense of ownership and agency in the digital realm. This model exemplifies how collective efforts at the grassroots level can catalyze broader systemic change, aligning with Dr. Rees's vision of a future where digital freedom is a shared pursuit.

Transition to Next Steps

As we synthesize these insights into a collective vision for digital freedom, it becomes clear that the path forward requires concerted effort, innovative thinking, and unwavering commitment to principles of equity and justice. The stories shared and the frameworks discussed here lay the groundwork for actionable strategies in the chapters to come. These strategies will focus on future-oriented approaches to continue advancing digital rights in an ever-shifting technological landscape. By embracing the potential for collaboration and cross-pollination of ideas, we move closer to realizing a world where connectivity serves as an unwavering lifeline for all.

As we reach the conclusion of Chapter 9, "Voices from the Frontier," we stand at the intersection of diverse perspectives and pivotal insights that seek to redefine the boundaries of digital rights. Through the tapestry of expert voices from multiple disciplines, we have gleaned the multifaceted nature of digital human rights, an area that demands our collective attention and action. Society is transforming under the weight of rapidly advancing technology, reshaping norms, and providing both opportunities for, and barriers to, inclusive participation.

The societal impacts of digital technology remind us that while digital rights can act as catalysts for democratic engagement and social movements, they also underline the urgency of addressing digital exclusion. Meanwhile, the ethical challenges presented by our hyper-connected world call for vigilant stewardship. As we navigate issues such as data privacy and algorithmic bias, the responsibility rests on all of us, individuals, corporations, and governments, to uphold digital ethics.

New technological innovations promise profound advancements and yet pose new challenges. Here, we are urged to consider how we can leverage technologies like artificial intelligence to champion digital empowerment, ensuring equitable access while preventing new forms of disparity.

The chapter's final call for a collective vision of digital freedom encapsulates the essence of our journey, an invitation to partner across sectors and geographies in pursuit of shared goals. As we transition to the book's conclusive section on future strategies, let us carry forth the understanding and motivation drawn from these discussions. In doing so, we empower ourselves to become active participants in bridging the digital divide, realizing a future where digital rights underpin both justice and equity for all.

CONCLUSION

As we stand on the threshold of an era where digital connectivity intricately weaves through every fiber of our societal fabric, we are presented with a profound opportunity, and responsibility, to redefine freedom itself. Throughout "Connected Rights: Reimagining Human Freedom in the Digital Age," we have charted the transformative journey of human rights as they dynamically evolve to meet the demands of the digital age. From historical underpinnings to the philosophical, ethical, and legal ramifications of digital rights, this book has painted a comprehensive portrait of the challenges and prospects we face.

Our exploration reveals that the integration of digital connectivity into the lexicon of basic human rights is not merely an academic notion but a crucial step towards genuine equity and empowerment. By acknowledging the internet as a pivotal enabler of human agency, we take bold strides toward addressing global disparities, ensuring everyone can partake in the opportunities it affords.

Transforming this vision into reality demands more than passive acknowledgment, it necessitates active participation from each of us. By embracing the strategies and concepts articulated in these pages, readers can significantly drive change within their personal and professional realms. Whether it's advocating for inclusive policies, spearheading initiatives that bridge the digital divide, or nurturing digital literacy, the potential for impactful transformation is boundless.

Now is the moment to transition from introspection to action. We must seize our roles as proactive architects of this new digital frontier. Let us commit to being steadfast advocates for digital rights, understanding that our collective efforts will lay the foundation for a future where connectivity knows no boundaries. Reach out to policymakers, collaborate with corporations, engage with community leaders, your voice and actions are paramount.

As we close this chapter, envision a world where every individual, irrespective of geography or circumstance, can leverage the global digital network to elevate their dreams. Together, we can propel humanity toward a future where interconnectedness transcends its technical constraints, becoming a universal bridge to opportunity and enlightenment. With purpose and passion, let us forge ahead, committed to envisioning and enacting a future defined by acceptance, accessibility, and enduring freedom.

Acknowledgments

Completing "Connected Rights: Reimagining Human Freedom in the Digital Age" has been an intricate journey of discovery, reflection, and growth, one that would not have been possible without the dedication and passion that have fueled my career. This book is the culmination of countless hours spent in reflection and research, motivated by the core belief that digital rights are, at their essence, human rights. Through this work, I hope to empower others to recognize and claim their own freedom in this increasingly interconnected world.

I extend heartfelt gratitude to the thought leaders whose remarkable contributions have shaped my understanding of this complex domain. To Tim Berners-Lee, whose invention of the World Wide Web opened the gates of digital freedom; to Lawrence Lessig, for his unyielding advocacy of digital rights and open access; and to Shoshana Zuboff, whose critical insight into surveillance capitalism has illuminated new paths for digital ethics. Their pioneering work continues to inspire me, providing a rich tapestry of ideas that challenge and motivate.

This journey would have been impossible without the unwavering support of my family and friends. My deepest thanks to my partner, who has been a constant source of encouragement and understanding, offering patience and love through late-night revisions and weekend brainstorming sessions. To my close friends, whose confidence and belief in my work never wavered, thank you for lifting me up.

I am incredibly grateful to the brilliant minds that make up my professional network, especially my editorial team. Your keen eyes and thoughtful feedback have refined my words and sharpened my vision, this book is as much a reflection of your talents as it is mine. Special thanks to my agent, whose strategic insight and tireless advocacy brought this project to life.

Finally, to you, the reader: may this book inspire you to listen for the voices of inspiration and cleave to the networks of support that propel us all toward a brighter digital future. Remember that every innovation is founded on perseverance and the shared wisdom of those who have come before us. As you engage with this text, I urge you to recognize and cherish those who empower you to grow and thrive. Together, we shape the narrative of human freedom in this digital age.

Author Biography

Dr. Eleanor Rees stands as a beacon of insight and advocacy in the expanding realm of digital rights, pioneering the notion that internet access is integral to the framework of modern human rights. Her journey began in the intellectually rich environment of Bristol, England, a city synonymous with technological advancement and scholarly pursuits. This vibrant backdrop kindled Eleanor's fascination with the power of connectivity, a theme that has become the leitmotif of her illustrious career.

With a doctorate in Digital Anthropology from the prestigious University of Oxford, Dr. Rees carved a niche exploring the intricate ties between human societies and advancing technologies. Her academic foray equipped her with an analytical repertoire that seamlessly blends rigorous scholarship with compelling storytelling. This unique synthesis has become the hallmark of her writing, championing the cause of global connectivity with both intellectual rigor and narrative warmth.

Eleanor's professional saga spans continents and cultures, reflecting her commitment to understanding and illuminating the digital divide's far-reaching impacts. Through her acclaimed works such as "Digital Lifelines: How the Internet Became a Human Right" and "The Global Digital Divide: Bridging the Last Frontier," she articulates a vision where the internet serves as an equitable channel for empowerment and social justice. Her explorations into remote villages and bustling cities alike have enriched her narrative with vibrant accounts of innovation and resilience.

Positioned at the confluence of tradition and progress, Eleanor's voice bridges the old and new worlds, making her an authoritative figure shaping the discourse on digital ethics and rights. Her books not only enhance readers' understanding of digital issues but also call them to participate actively in the quest for universal connectivity. Dr. Rees's work thus transcends the page, inspiring readers and stakeholders alike to envision a future defined by inclusive and equitable digital landscapes.

Sources of Content

The insights and methodologies presented in "Connected Rights: Reimagining Human Freedom in the Digital Age" spring from a robust confluence of practical experience, foundational principles, and emerging trends in the digital sphere. Dr. Eleanor Rees, with her extensive background in digital anthropology and global connectivity, anchors the book in her professional expertise and first-hand experiences. Her comprehensive understanding of how digital rights intersect with human rights forms the bedrock upon which the book's strategies and analyses are built.

The content of the book is further enriched through a meticulous analysis of sector-specific practices, business models, and the dynamic tendencies shaping the industry. Dr. Rees leverages a wide range of real-world applications and case studies to ground her arguments in tangible examples, illustrating the book's core thesis with clarity and precision. By engaging readers through these practical lenses, she ensures that the insights are both actionable and deeply relevant.

Additionally, the developmental process behind the book has been augmented by cutting-edge AI tools, including generative analyses using platforms such as ChatGPT. This integration allows for an expansive exploration of relevant sources and examples, enabling the narrative to incorporate diverse perspectives and case-based learning. The melding of Dr. Rees's professional insights with this innovative editorial technology results in a compelling narrative that not only informs but also inspires action within the digital rights discourse. Through this synthesis, "Connected Rights" emerges as both a scholarly and practical guide, positioning itself as a vital resource in the ongoing dialogue about digital freedom and equity.

www.ingramcontent.com/pod-product-compliance
Lightning Source LLC
La Vergne TN
LVHW051323050326
832903LV00031B/3327